Lost Boy,
Lost Girl

Lost Boy, Lost Girl

ESCAPING CIVIL WAR IN SUDAN

By John Bul Dau and Martha Arual Akech

With Michael S. Sweeney and K. M. Kostyal

NATIONAL GEOGRAPHIC

WASHINGTON, D.C.

To our lovely Children; Agot, Leek, and our three-day-old daughter, Akur. This book is dedicated to you. When you are able to read on your own, it should act as an introduction to the ordeals that your mother and I went through. You are sweet kids, and we thank Almighty God for keeping us alive during the war, a time when we never thought we would survive to even have children! —j&m

Table of Contents

Part One

PEACE

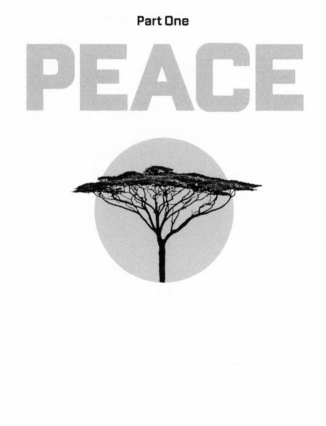

John

When I was a young boy, my great-uncle Aleer-Manguak was killed while trying to protect our cattle from a lion. His bravery made me proud.

My people, the Dinka, raise cows in Southern Sudan. We like to drink their milk, and we use them as a form of money. Protecting our precious cows from predators is a constant problem. Sometimes we must kill or be killed.

One day five lions sneaked into the pastures near Paguith, my first village. Lions are smart and work in groups. If they want to attack a herd, they first try to make the cows panic. They sometimes do this by creeping near the cattle and spreading their urine on the ground. Then they quietly move to the opposite side of the herd. When the cows wander far enough to sniff the odor of lion urine, they know a killer is nearby and run in the opposite direction—right toward the waiting lions. This is exactly what happened that day. Hundreds of cows ran into the trap, and two fell to the lions' fangs and claws. My brother and some other Dinka boys saw what happened and tried to chase the lions away. They ran at the lions and threw sticks to drive them from their kill. That just made the lions angry. Some of them turned on the boys, and they had to run for their lives.

The boys hurried to the village and alerted everyone that lions had attacked the cattle. The women of the village began to shout, and the men began to arm themselves. My father and great-uncle got their knives and spears and left their houses to meet the other men of the village. They quickly decided to form a hunting party. They would have gone after the lions right then, but night had begun to fall and they had to suspend their pursuit. Everyone went to bed anxious for the hunt to begin. After the sun rose the next morning, a hunting party that had special skills in tracking lions began to follow their path. About thirty men, all armed with spears, set off after the trackers through the tall grass.

By the time they found the lions, two had run off, but three remained in the thick grass and brush. The hunters circled them and began to walk toward each other, drawing the circle smaller and smaller. Two of the three lions didn't want anything to do with the Dinka hunters and escaped through gaps in the circle. That left one. He was a big male with a broad face and a golden mane.

Remember how I said lions are smart? This one certainly was. He did not want to tangle with humans and was trying to keep his distance, but the shrinking circle gave him no chance to flee. The lion began to get nervous. To get close enough to actually kill the lion, the hunters needed to create a distraction. The Dinka say, "Who is going to bring the lion?" It is a special kind of job. The bringer stabs the lion to make it angry. The lion then chases its attacker, who runs for his life. The fastest runners in the village train to "bring the lion." My great-uncle was one of them.

As the men of my village knelt with their spears pointed at the center of the circle, Aleer-Manguak and another runner rushed straight at the lion. As they sped by, they stabbed the great beast with the tips of their spears. The lion roared in anger and pain. It rose on all four legs and chased Aleer-Manguak. The beast caught him just as he reached the circle of hunters. It swiped at him with one paw, tearing open his shoulder and breaking his ribs. The other hunters swarmed over the lion and pierced its flesh with their spears, killing it quickly. My great-uncle lived just a little while longer, and then he died too.

The entire village honored my great-uncle. The hunters took the lion's body and cut off the tail, paws, and mane. They gave these to Aleer-Manguak's family as tokens of respect for his brave deed and his self-sacrifice. The family hung the prizes in their luak, a round Dinka cattle pen with a thatched roof.

Even as a boy of seven or eight, I knew why everyone honored Aleer-Manguak in death. Almost from birth, a child is taught the values of the Dinka, which my great-uncle had in abundance. These values include respect, courage, hard work, and self-sacrifice. A Dinka child is also taught to fight for family, village, tribe, and country. The strongest fighters are those who keep two rules. First, they never, ever give up, no matter what the odds are against them. And second, like the lions, they work together. A Dinka man who follows these rules and maintains the values he learned as a boy can grow up to be a great leader, like my great-uncle. At the time I had no idea how much I would have to live by these rules just to survive the ordeals of my life. Aside from the occasional marauding visit by a lion or hyena, my childhood years were peaceful and fun.

Nobody kept exact records in Southern Sudan, but my family believes that I was born in July 1974. My father was Deng Leek Deng Aleer. He had been a mighty wrestler when he was young and later became a judge. He did not go to school to learn the law. Instead, we Dinka say that he held the laws in his heart. He knew our traditions and our values and was called upon to settle disputes. He disciplined me severely when I was young, especially if I showed any disrespect. At the time I thought he was too strict, but now I realize that he was raising me to be strong, as a Dinka man should be.

My mother was Anon Manyok Duot Lual. She was the daughter of a Dinka chief and was considered quite an excellent bride. My father had to pay many cows to her male relatives as a sign of his respect before he could marry her and give their children his name. It is common among the Dinka for a man to have more than one wife. After my father married my mother, he took three more wives, and he had many children. I am the youngest son of my mother.

Like all good Dinka, my family raised cattle. These are not the cows you see on North American farms. Dinka cows look wilder than their American cousins and have thick horns that are two to three feet long. Their milk is sweet, and we drink it all the time.

We slaughter a cow for its meat only to mark a big occasion. We believe that cows are a gift from God.

Our legends say that God offered the first Dinka man a choice between the gift of the first cow and a secret gift, called the "What." God told the first man to carefully consider his choice. The secret gift was very great, God said, but he would not reveal anything more about it. The first man looked at the cow and thought it was a very good gift. "If you insist on having the cow, then I advise you to taste her milk before you decide," God said. The first man tried the milk and liked it. He considered the choice and picked the cow. He never saw the secret gift. God gave that gift to others.

The Dinka believe that the secret gift went to the people of the West. It helped them invent and explore and build and become strong. Meanwhile, the Dinka never built factories or highways or cars or planes. They were content to be farmers and cattle raisers. They lived happily for centuries, drinking milk and using cows as currency. Cows remain the lifeblood of the Dinka culture.

Narrow dirt paths link one village with another all over Southern Sudan. There are no paved roads and virtually no buildings of metal or brick. Mud, sticks, leaves, and grass are our construction materials. There are no phones, no computers, no cars, no kitchen appliances—virtually none of the conveniences that many people in the world take for granted. Our culture has not changed much in hundreds of years, and we like it that way.

Southern Sudan is very flat. The land is covered with grass that grows eight feet high between patches of forest and farmland. The year follows seasons of rain and drought. When it rains, the flat lands fill with standing water and our villages become like swamps. When the rains stop, the land dries to dust and the sun burns very, very hot. Some lands—in an area called the Sudd that separates Northern and Southern Sudan—never go dry. Even late in the dry season, these lands hold enough water to grow grasses to feed our cattle. Beyond those swampy lands is the White Nile River. It has crocodiles, mosquitoes, and hippopotamuses. For many centuries, the swamp and the dangerous animals that live in it served as a barrier to people who wanted to explore Southern Sudan. That's why the Dinka lived in isolation until the nineteenth century, when British explorers and missionaries began pushing through the swamp.

My father's father's brother was a great man. His name was Deng Malual Aleer. He was a big chief in Southern Sudan and fought on the side of the British colonizers against the Arabs who lived in Northern Sudan and wanted to control the whole country. He gave permission for missionaries to do their work in the southernmost part of Sudan, and that is how my family became Christians. Because of Dinka traditions and the work of the missionaries, I have two names. My traditional Dinka name is Dhieu-Deng Leek (pronounced "Lake"). I also am known by my Christian name, John Bul Dau. Many Dinka families give their children a name from the Bible when they are baptized, and that is how I became John at age four or five.

Like all Dinka children, I had to do chores from a very early age. I got up when the red circle of the sun cleared the horizon. Every morning, I went immediately to our luak with my brothers to lead our cows outside. When the luak was empty, we cleaned the floor. We gathered up the dung from the night before and hauled it outside. Then we broke it into tiny bits to dry in the sun. We burned the dried dung every day. It gave off a smelly smoke that protected our cows from biting flies and other pests.

Meanwhile, my father and mother tended to their garden, cutting weeds from their patches of corn, beans, sorghum, and pumpkins. Mother took a break around midday to make a lunch of thin griddle cakes. The older boys kept watch over the cattle, while my friends and I played with our toys. We did not have fancy playthings that make noise when you push a button. We made toy cows out of clay and made the sounds of cows and goats with our mouths. We had fun pretending to run our own farms. We also played a running game called *alueth*. It's played with two bases, one for someone taking the role of a lion and the other for children whom the lion "hunts." The children leave one base and run toward the safety of the other. If the lion catches a child between the bases, he joins the lion's team. As more and more children become "lions," it gets harder and harder for the remaining children to avoid getting captured.

Once I was old enough, I went with the older boys to protect the cattle as they grazed on the thick grasses around our village. Like the other boys, I learned how to fight with knives and spears and clubs. I wrestled with my friends until I grew strong and tall. My friends and I prided ourselves on learning how to throw one another to the ground and on mastering the many moves of a champion wrestler.

I didn't go to school. The only schools were in the biggest of villages, far away, or in the northern part of Sudan, where people spoke Arabic. Instead, I learned what I needed to know through the rituals of storytelling. Everyone played games with riddles, shared stories among the family after dinner at the end of the day, and told stories at cattle camp, a grassy place away from home where villagers tended their precious cows. Our stories and riddles not only taught us about the animals and plants and people of our world, but they also bathed us in lessons of right and wrong. When we heard stories about hyena, for example, we learned how his greedy, self-centered ways caused him many problems. We learned that we wanted to be more like the noble eagle, the smart fox, and the powerful elephant.

Every night my brothers and sisters and I told each other tales we had heard during the day, and we begged our parents to share with us the older stories from when people and animals lived together and spoke to one another. Then my mother checked to be sure the doors and windows had been sealed against the clouds of mosquitoes outside, and we lay on our beds of cowhide. Our village had no electricity, and our daytime cooking fires burned too low at night to give off any light, so each night brought nearly total darkness to the inside of our house and luak. Night after night I drifted off to sleep, never dreaming how soon our beautiful storytelling evenings would end.

Martha

I didn't grow up in the countryside, the way John did. I grew up in Juba, the most important city in Southern Sudan. My family—my father, my mother, my little sister, Tabitha, and I—lived in a compound with another family. Our house had a roof made of dried, thatched grasses and three rooms—a kitchen and two small rooms where we slept and, during the long rainy season, where we played. During the hot, dry season, everybody would bring chairs outside and sit in the shade. Despite the sweltering heat of the Equator, Sudanese people spend most of their time outdoors when it's not raining.

On dry season evenings, when it was cooler, all of us children in the neighborhood would gather together to play tag. Sometimes we girls pretended that we were cooking, and we'd make plates and cooking pots out of clay, the way Sudanese women do. Or we played with dolls our mothers had made us out of scraps of old clothing.

My father was a policeman, but early in the morning before he went to work and before the scorching sun was very high in the sky, he and my mother would take Tabitha and me with them while they worked in a garden they had not far from our house. They grew mostly groundnuts. You call them peanuts, and we eat them just the way you do, as snacks or in peanut butter, which we also put in sauces or in our porridge.

Juba was a major port city on the great Nile. The longest river in the world, the Nile flows through the length of Sudan, then through Egypt to the Mediterranean Sea. Large boats heading south on the Nile couldn't go any farther than Juba because of the rapids and shallows on the upper part of the river, so that made my town a busy port. Still, most of the roads in town were unpaved, and in the dry season, the dust kicked up by cattle being herded through town or by farm carts loaded with vegetables swirled through the air. In the rainy season, the roads were a muddy mess. The main paved road in town had been put in by the British when Sudan was a colony of theirs.

Sudan is the largest country in Africa, and there are hundreds of groups, or tribes, and many languages spoken throughout it. Like John, I am part of the Dinka people, the biggest tribe in Southern Sudan. Besides my tribe, I also belong to a clan. This is like a large, extended family whose members help one another. If you are Dinka, your clan is very important to your identity. John's clan is the Bor Nyarweng. Mine is the Abek. My Dinka first name is Arual, the name my father's family gives to firstborn girls.

My parents were Christians, and on Sundays we went to

church. Before Christianity came to Southern Sudan, people there believed in witches, and they thought that illnesses came from being cursed or bewitched. Those beliefs still lingered when I was a child, even in cities like Juba.

Once, when my younger sister, Tabitha, was quite little, she got very sick. We could see where each bone in her body was connected because she was so thin. Friends of my mother's said that her baby had been cursed. They told my mother that she needed to find a witch doctor to get rid of the curse. At first, she said, "No, I'm a Christian. I don't believe in those things." But when Tabitha got worse, my mother became frantic and gave in. She found a witch doctor who came and looked at poor little Tabitha.

"Someone has put magical bones on her body, and they're killing her," he pronounced. He said that only he could see the magical bones and only he could get them off. So my mother, in her desperation, hired him. But every time he came, he would leave Tabitha in her sick bed and walk around outside our compound.

Now in Juba there were no trash collectors, so people threw their trash outside the fences that surrounded their homes. When the witch doctor walked around outside, he would come back and lean over Tabitha and suddenly pull some kind of bone away from her. To my mother, those bones looked suspiciously like garbage people had thrown away. "Go away, and don't come back," she told him. Instead she prayed that God would heal her baby, and after some time, Tabitha recovered.

I was a little child then, too little to understand how sick my sister was. Also, like all small children, I thought my parents would always keep us safe. Most of what I remember from my first five years in Juba was the happy sound of people in my family and neighborhood. My parents loved me, and every night when I crawled into my nice metal bed with the comfortable mattress on it, the world seemed like a good place.

I didn't understand that Southern Sudan had been a dangerous place for decades. When my parents were children, there had been a war between the southerners and the Arab Muslims who dominated the government in Sudan. That war ended with a treaty, and for ten years peace had kept life calm and allowed people to settle and prosper. But trouble started brewing again just after I was born.

The southern people were angry with the Arab government about a number of things. One was that the government planned to build a canal into the great swamp called the Sudd. The canal would carry the water away from the south to the Arab Muslims in the north and on to Egypt. Also, prices of critical supplies such as oil, bread, and sugar had risen because of the policies of the government in the capital city of Khartoum. Most important, the government had imposed Muslim law on the whole country, even though we black Africans of the south weren't Muslim. The Arabs had never had much respect for us. They treated us as if we were beneath them, as if we were their servants.

In Juba and in other cities students protested against the government, and some were killed in the riots. Men in the south who were fed up with policies that favored the north formed the Sudan People's Liberation Army, and fighting flared in the countryside between the SPLA, as we called that army, and local militia groups that the government had backed. But I wasn't paying attention to any of that. I was just a girl of five, playing with my sister and my friends, expecting life to go on the way it was forever.

Part Two

WAR

John

War came to my homeland when I was thirteen years old. We had been expecting it, but nevertheless it came as a shock when my village was actually attacked.

The Dinka had heard omens of war for a long time. Many people still believed in spirits that lived in animals and plants, and these spirits spoke to them about the coming of a very bad time. My parents told me one story just as they had heard it. They said a tortoise spoke to a man on a path outside the town of Bor. Among the Dinka, the tortoise is believed to be very smart. The tortoise told the man, "I am sent by the Lord. I bring you news of doom. Your country, Southern Sudan, will be destroyed." The tortoise said the Lord meant to punish the people of Southern Sudan for being unfaithful, and it gave the man three choices. "One is drought," said the tortoise, "and if you choose it, I will punish you by withholding the rain. If you do not choose that, I will punish you with flood. And if you do not choose that, I will punish you with war.

Now, you must choose." The man was frightened and ran away. The tortoise yelled at him, saying, "You must answer me! You must choose!" So the man chose war.

The man told everyone what the tortoise had said. The people of Duk Payuel, the village where my family was living at the time, debated whether the man had made a wise choice. Some argued in favor of drought. They knew they could survive because the Dinka have weathered many a dry spell. But drought meant famine, which would hit the women and children the hardest, so the villagers rejected that choice. Some argued in favor of flood. They knew the Dinka could survive because they could catch fish as the swamps filled with water. But floods meant our precious cows would die, so the villagers rejected that choice too. Most of the people in my village finally decided that the man had chosen wisely, but everyone kept talking about what the tortoise had said.

A month or two later, a crow landed on the shoulder of an old woman who was sitting making rope in the shade of her house. The crow gave her the same choice: drought, flood, or war. The woman didn't know what to do, so she said nothing. The crow flew away.

Then a prophet had a vision. This man, named Ngun Deng, lived among the Nuer, a neighboring tribe. He saw bad things in the future. War would come to Southern Sudan, he said, and many would die. In the end, Southern Sudan would defeat the enemy, but it also would suffer defeat. Then he spoke a final prophecy: "Yours will be a generation of black hair." The elders in my village debated his meaning. They decided he meant that the oldest and youngest would die. The oldest had gray or white hair, and the youngest had little or no hair. Only the black-haired young people would live, and they would see many troubles.

It was such a terrible time. People believed the words of the tortoise, the crow, and the prophet. Then one day the sun glowed blood red. My mother said it meant that blood would flow. "People will fight, and there will be lots of killing," she told me.

At the time, I did not know much about my country's history. Anyone who studied the early years of Sudan might have seen civil war in its future. Britain granted Sudan independence in 1956. The new nation brought together groups of people who had little in common. Arabs who practiced Islam and spoke Arabic dominated the northern half of Sudan and the capital, Khartoum. Black-skinned tribes who were either Christian or practiced traditional religions and who spoke dozens of languages dominated the southern half. At first, southern citizens saw little change in their daily lives while living in their new country. In the early 1980s, however, when the national government, dominated by northern Arabs, tried to impose Islamic laws on the entire nation, civil war broke out. Northern soldiers stormed into southern villages to quell the violence, but the fighting raged on. The northern armies got the best of most battles because they had more soldiers and guns and all of the airplanes. Those armies drew near shortly after we heard the prophecies of war.

I remember the night the soldiers came to Duk Payuel as if it were yesterday. The first sound I heard seemed like a low whine or whistle. It rose from far away on a moonless evening as I tried to sleep on the floor of a hut. About a dozen boys and girls shared the hut with me on that hot and sticky summer night in 1987. As government soldiers shelled and burned the countryside and airplanes strafed and bombed the villages, refugees moved south. Some came to Duk Payuel, and that is how I came to share a hut with strangers. My parents and other adults slept on the ground outside.

I was having trouble sleeping, so I heard clearly the whine or whistle as it grew louder. Then I heard more sounds just like the first. A chorus of shrieks descended toward our village.

Boom! Boom! Boom! Explosions shook the earth. I heard a huge crackling sound like some giant tree being splintered in the forest. I had learned enough from the elders who had gathered in our village to realize what was happening. Duk Payuel was being shelled by invaders.

I stood up and tried to run, but it was so dark in the hut that I could only stumble about. Other children were running too, and we smacked into each other and into the walls and support beams. Outside, amid a new sound that I recognized as bursts of gunfire, my mother shrieked the names of her children. I managed to find my way outdoors and looked up to see the red glare of fire dancing atop the trees of the forest and the roofs of our village. Everywhere, people were running in a mad panic. Bullets tore through the village, making angry zipping sounds like bees.

I looked for my parents and my brothers and sisters, but I

saw no family members. I started to panic. Where should I go to be safe? Thank goodness, just then I thought I saw my father running in front of me. He disappeared down a path through the tall grass, and I followed him. I ran and ran but did not see him. Suddenly a hand reached out from the thick grass at the side of the path and grabbed my shoulder. As I felt myself being pulled into the grass, I heard a hoarse whisper.

"Quiet, quiet, quiet," it said.

Nine northern soldiers dressed in dark clothes ran along the path I had just left, passing inches from my face without seeing me. They fired their guns as they went. The two of us backed deeper into the grass. We did not say anything, just crouched and waited for daybreak.

When it came, I was shocked. The soldiers had gone. My village was destroyed. I could see smoking ruins of huts and luaks, dead animals, and bodies of villagers whom the adults were trying to hide from the eyes of children. And I could see by the early morning light that the man who had saved me was not my father. He was Abraham, a neighbor. My family was missing, and I felt certain they had been killed or taken prisoner.

Abraham said we would have to flee if we wanted to stay alive. The soldiers from the north would probably kill us if they found us. Our best chance for survival lay in finding somewhere the soldiers could not hurt us. I did not know how tough our journey would be, but I knew we did not have much in our favor. We had no food or water. I wore what I had worn to bed, which is to say I was naked. As we fled we might encounter more soldiers, not to mention deserts and jungles and the dangers that lurk there.

Abraham and I ran toward the east and the rising sun. We kept to the paths that serve as roads in Southern Sudan. Every time we heard approaching feet we ducked into the brush. When the noise passed by, we emerged and started running again. For a while we traveled with three other refugees from the invading army, a Dinka woman and her two daughters. We had nothing to eat for a long time until Abraham found a pumpkin and an *amochro*, a short plant with a fleshy, juicy root shaped like an onion. The girls complained of being tired from walking so much, and I was very tired too. My bare feet bled, and my stomach growled after the food ran out. But we kept going toward the east.

One day, as Abraham was leading us single-file along the path, he disappeared around a curve. When we caught up to him, we saw he had stopped near a group of soldiers carrying assault rifles. Abraham was wearing a nice shirt, and the men ordered him to give it up. When Abraham hesitated, the men pummeled him with sticks and the butts of their rifles until he took off the shirt and offered it to the officer in charge. The soldiers beat the woman too. I wanted to cry out, but I thought it best to stay silent. Then one of the soldiers grabbed a clump of my hair and twisted. Tears came to my eyes, but I willed myself not to cry out. The man tore a clump of my hair out by the roots and threw it in my face. That seemed to satisfy him, and he stopped picking on me. We lay in pain by the path and said nothing. Eventually the soldiers got tired of torturing us and moved on.

We saw other people from time to time. One group of soldiers beat Abraham until he almost died, and also punched me and hit me with sticks. They took the woman and her two daughters with them when they left. We never saw them again. It took a long time to recover from this vicious beating, but Abraham and I grew strong enough to walk again. I remember those days as a blur. We did nothing but walk like zombies, stumbling along and searching for food. All the while we headed east. I wanted to quit, but Abraham insisted we could not stop.

"We will keep going until we are killed," Abraham said.

I learned then that we had a destination: Ethiopia. It was a separate country east of Sudan. We would have to walk about five hundred miles to reach its border. Frankly, I did not believe we would make it. Every morning when I awoke hungry and sore, I thought it might be the day I would die. Facing the threat of starvation, thirst, and murderous soldiers, I looked upon our long walk as a sort of grim game. The object was to see how far we could get before we died. I prayed I would live long enough to learn what had happened to my family.

As we walked, Abraham told me stories. He taught me how to find a kind of grass called *apai* and how to chew its sweet stems for food. He taught me to beware of water holes because they attract animals and people. And he taught me the best ways to hide. This last lesson came in handy when a group of soldiers nearly found us along a riverbank. We had stopped at a big river covered with apai.

Abraham and I had picked our apai and submerged our bodies comfortably in the water as we chewed.

Only a minute or two after we settled in, I heard voices speaking in Arabic, along with gunshots and laughter. I was very scared, but I kept still and hid amid the apai. I grabbed some roots on the bottom of the river and pulled myself slowly down until only my lips and nose were above water. Abraham did exactly the same thing. We breathed as quietly as we could and watched the men through the muddy water that covered our eyes.

A squad of Arabs stood on the bank a few yards from where I hid. They fired their guns in the air in their joy at having found water, and they shouted "Allah akbar!" which means "God is great!" Some sat and smoked tobacco. Some prayed. One man urinated in the water not far from me. Some even jumped in the water and splashed about. The waves they made rocked me as I tried to stay hidden.

After an hour or so, an officer blew a whistle and everyone jumped to attention. Then they marched past us and went on their way. Thus ended the longest hour of my life. When I felt sure they were gone, I emerged from the water. Abraham came out too. We ran into the forest, where we felt temporarily safe. When we had calmed down, we started walking again.

In the following weeks, we met other refugees. It became clear that lots of people were fleeing the war by walking to Ethiopia. Many died from gunshots, thirst, and hunger, but Abraham and I continued on. We met fifteen boys and two adults along the way, and we all decided to walk together.

By the end of October, the land was getting to be very dry. We had nothing to drink. Some of the boys said they wanted to die. Some tried to cry, but no tears came. We were so thirsty that we ate mud to force some moisture into our mouths, but it did not really help. I was so afraid I would die that I gladly drank urine to stay alive. I sang to try to keep my spirits up, but it did not help much. "Don't let your heart get upset," I sang to myself. "You are in the hand of God."

The group that joined us began to dwindle away. Some died of thirst and hunger, and the two adults were shot when we ran into an ambush. Finally, only Abraham and I and two of the other boys remained. We kept walking with nothing to eat or drink. But at the moment of my greatest despair, we found hope. Abraham disappeared ahead of us. When he returned, he brought water in his cupped hands. I drank and knew I would survive. Right around the corner was the huge Kangen Swamp. We caught and cooked some turtles and ate their flesh and their eggs. I drank muddy swamp water. It tasted great.

Not long after that we came to the border of Ethiopia. Members of a friendly tribe on the Sudanese side gave us a blanket, some elephant meat, and some advice. They told us to cross into Ethiopia and head for a refugee camp called Pinyudu. So that is where we went.

Martha

I was a little girl, not even six years old, when the happy days with my family in Juba disappeared forever. It all started when my mother and my little sister and I left our home and went to stay with my grandmother and my aunt's family. They lived in a farming and cattle-raising village in the countryside. But it wasn't really my home, and I got scared when my mother left us there and went back to Juba. When she returned to us, she brought a lot of our belongings with her—things like clothes and cooking pots and utensils.

When you are little and in the arms of your family, you don't really understand, or even care, what's going on in the rest of the world. Now I know, though, that my parents moved us away from Juba because war had broken out in Southern Sudan, and everyone expected that Juba would become the scene of fierce fighting between government-backed troops and the SPLA.

By Dinka custom, families move to places where the father has relatives. That meant we couldn't stay with my mother's mother and sister for very long. So we moved again, this time to a village called Wernyol, where my father had been born. A little later he joined us there.

We stayed in my uncle's house there for a few months because we had no house of our own anymore. Then my father's relatives held a feast and killed a cow to roast and invited a lot of people to come and enjoy the meat and help us build a new house. As the delicious smell of meat cooking drifted through the air, everybody worked together, and soon we had a small house with mud walls and a thatched roof and a garden for vegetables nearby. My family was all together again and we had our own home, so it seemed that all was well.

We discovered that life in the country was different from life in the city. We had to keep all our food safe from rats and mice and cats, so the women wove grass baskets for storage. Or they would cut the top off a big gourd they had grown and use that, sticking an ear of corn in the opening to seal it. There are some gourds that grow perfectly round, and we would cut these in half and use them as plates. Other gourds we used as drinking cups. People carved spoons from wood, or we collected empty snail shells, which make really good spoons. Cooking pots were made out of clay and shaped by hand. All the women knew how to do this, but some people were so good at it that they could sell their pots. Not for money—there was no money. Instead they might get a big container of corn or a cow.

My mother had given Tabitha a metal spoon, a leftover from our life in Juba. Tabitha treasured that spoon and always hid it inside the luak, the cattle shed, under a log that supported the wall. One day, when it was time to eat, she went to get it, and when she reached under the log, a snake bit her! She was screaming and screaming. We watched that big long snake slither away, but luckily it wasn't poisonous. We always had to be careful about snakes in the countryside. There were lots of them. We even saw a mad cobra in the yard. It was rearing up, taller than we were. We ran and ran, as far from it as we could get.

One afternoon, my parents went to church in a nearby village and left Tabitha and me behind with my father's cousin, a woman named Nyanriak. It was a nice, quiet afternoon, with cattle grazing in front of the family compound and Nyanriak in the yard grinding millet—a kind of grain we Dinka eat a lot. We were playing with other kids in the sunshine when all of a sudden we heard gunfire, and Nyanriak yelled at us, "You children, *come here, come here!*" We went running toward her and she pushed us toward the luak. We were screaming, "The Murle are coming. The Murle are coming."

The Murle are another tribe in Southern Sudan, and we knew about them because they would raid villages and steal not only cattle but Dinka children, whom they would raise as their own. It was said they couldn't have children themselves, and that's why they did this. Whenever a village heard gunfire, the first thought in everyone's mind was that the Murle had come on a raid. But the Murle don't burn villages down, and now houses were on fire, and the world had become a big storm of smoke and gunfire and screaming. People were running toward us, shouting out the names of their children or shouting at us to *"Run! Run!"*

Nyanriak grabbed us and her five small children and herded us along with the crowd, prodding us to run as fast as our short legs would carry us. We raced after the other people leaving the village, running through tall grass high above our heads. The people ahead of us had made a path in the grass with their running, so we followed that, but sometimes we had to scramble through thorny bushes that scratched as we passed. We were barefoot, the way most Sudanese children are, and our feet grew big blisters on them, but we kept going as fast as we could. I was holding Tabitha's hand the whole time. She was only three and not much of a runner. But then neither was I.

At last, at dark we rested near a pool of water where we could drink and cool our aching feet. We hadn't gotten separated from Nyanriak and her children, thank goodness, and now we were with a bigger group of people from our village. That group would become our new family.

We had no food to eat, as everybody had run away from the village with just the clothes on their backs. Besides being hungry, we were so tired and our feet hurt so much. The adults let us sleep for a couple of hours before we moved on. Tabitha and I curled up next to each other on the ground. I was too scared and shocked to understand it then, but now I think of that night as the beginning of a bad dream that would last for years. It was probably good that I didn't know what lay ahead for Tabitha and me.

As soon as dawn lightened the sky, we moved on. The adults were afraid the government-backed militia that had attacked us could still be nearby, and they wanted to keep us moving as fast as we could away from our village. Nyanriak had her own five kids to take care of, but she knew that Tabitha was too little to keep up with the rest of the group. She asked a man named Deng to take care of Tabitha. He often carried her on his shoulders. I followed close behind, watching Tabitha's feet dangling above my head as Deng marched along. I was always looking up to make sure that my little sister was safe.

The next day we came to a village, and the people there gave our group a gourd for water, dried kernels of corn to boil for food, and a pot to cook in. Such simple things, the gourd and the pot, but without them it was hard to eat or drink. We were thankful to the villagers and warned them that the militia was moving through the area, leaving death and destruction in their wake. In the weeks ahead, as we moved from village to village, we sounded the alarm, spreading warnings as we went.

As the fighting in the south grew worse and more villages were attacked, more and more people joined us, including elders who tried to keep everybody in line. For us Dinka, elders are the respected adults who guide us and care for us. When elders in our group saw a small child too tired to walk, they would carry the child. I wasn't carried very often, and I didn't want to be because I needed to follow whoever was carrying Tabitha. I began to feel that now I was her mother and responsible for keeping her safe.

After many days, we left all the villages behind and walked through an area covered in low forests for a while. The forest time had good and bad parts. It was cool in the shade of the trees, and some of the trees had leaves and fruits we could pick to eat. A few of the elders would go out and hunt the forest animals, too. If they managed to kill a deer or antelope, we'd make a fire and roast the meat. Anything was delicious because we were hungry all the time.

But I was also really afraid of the animals. In Sudan there are lots of wild animals, and people have to be very cautious. The whole time we were in the forest, I remembered a story my mother had told us. She had walked to another county once, hoping to trade some fabric she had sewn into filters for straining liquid in exchange for corn we could eat. At dusk, as she was walking back to our village alone, she entered a stand of tall trees and heard a big crack from a branch. She froze, then slowly looked over her shoulder and saw that a big cat, probably a leopard, had jumped out of the tree and was on the path behind her. But it was looking in the other direction! The wind must have been carrying her scent away from it, because it didn't turn around. She was shaking, but she slowly, quietly crept into the bushes to hide. Finally, the huge cat slunk away, and she ran home.

I also remembered another time, when I was at a cattle camp with my uncle and my mother and sister. A hyena came very close to us, but hyenas are easy to run off—at least if you're an adult. I had heard they would attack children, though. Now, at night in the forest, I remembered those dangers. Often we were on the move at night, when it was cooler and harder for any militias that might be around to spot us. But in the dark, we couldn't see where we were stepping. I kept worrying that when I took the next step, my bare foot would feel a snake slithering under it.

When we left the forest behind, the desert lay in front of us. Now there was no food to eat and no water to drink. When we came to a dry riverbed, people would dig and dig and dig, looking for wet mud to suck on. We ate that mud, too, as if it were food. A lot of people gave up hope, and we lost some of our group. And so many of us kids got sick. We felt so tired and ill that we'd find a spot to lie down and say to ourselves, "This is it, I'm not going to make it. I can't go on anymore." But somehow, most of us did make it. Whenever we found a little water, we'd drink too much at once and that made us sick. Since the water was dirty, it also gave us diarrhea and we felt even weaker.

When at last we came to a creek with plenty of water, I was very, very, very sick. I shivered so hard and was so weak with a fever that I couldn't move. I probably had a disease called malaria. Most of the people in my group got it at some time or other, because mosquitoes carry it and they were always pestering us.

So many of us were sick and exhausted that the elders decided our group should rest a few days by the creek. Some of the men went off to hunt and came back with meat to roast.

I was so sick that it was hard for me to eat. I just lay on the ground, and Tabitha sat beside me, staring at me. I could tell she was very scared because I couldn't take care of her, and that only made me feel worse.

After a few days, we broke up our camp and started to cross the creek. Suddenly, gunfire rained down on us from the few trees in our path. This time it really was the Murle! They were waiting to ambush us because we were in their territory and they thought we had killed their cattle to eat. They had seen the smoke from our fires and smelled roasting meat, so they had come looking for us.

In just a few minutes, they had killed five people and wounded others. The gunshots woke me out of my sick daze, and I started screaming and screaming and screaming. I couldn't stop. One man was lying on the path in front of us, dead and staring at the sky. Even today, when I close my eyes, I can see him lying there.

Our men started shooting back at the Murle, and they ran away, but we ran too, crossing the shallow creek and racing up the other side. The elders were trying to keep us from scattering everywhere and losing each other. I ran with Tabitha, and we didn't look back. The strange thing was that the whole terrible attack scared my sickness away, and I was able to keep going, even when we had to cross a muddy area, where we sank up to our knees and the elders had to drag us kids through the ooze.

Finally, we came to a little town where we could rest for a few days. Men from the SPLA were there, and the villagers gave us milk and millet and sorghum—a kind of grain you boil and eat like grits. Usually by the time we got it, the food was cold and had no taste, but we didn't care. When you're really hungry, your body just wants any kind of food to stay alive.

In that town, the big group that we had been with for weeks decided to split up. We had heard of two refugee camps in Ethiopia. One was closer than the other, but no one was sure if the United Nations (UN) was there with food and supplies to help us. The other, farther camp was called Pinyudu. I listened to the elders debate these camps back and forth among themselves. Some said the UN was at Pinyudu already, so it was worth going the extra distance. Our friend Deng was going there, but Nyanriak was worn out from being on the run with so many children, so she decided to go to the closer camp. She asked Deng if he would take Tabitha and me with him. She had her own five kids to take care of. Two more were just too much.

So it was decided. Tabitha and I would go with the group traveling to Pinyudu. We just followed what the adults told us to do. Of course we would. That was the tradition among the Dinka, to respect your elders and do what they told you. But even if our traditions had been different, I was six and Tabitha was three. What choice does any young child have but to do as the adults say?

For another week and a half or two we walked on. The days had run together for me a long time ago, so I wasn't even sure how long it had been since that terrible day when my parents went off to church and I saw them for the last time.

Once we crossed the border into Ethiopia, we were in forest again. The local people along the border, the Anyuak, were good to us, and we went from village to village. It was the growing season, May or June, and they had food to spare. These people were not cattle keepers like we Dinka, so they had no milk, but they gave us corn on the cob that we roasted or boiled and tomatoes and the leaves from a bean plant and lots of mangoes. It all tasted so good. I realized after a while that I had stopped being so afraid all the time. We were in a different kind of place, and I was curious about it and the people who lived there. And soon we would be in Pinyudu, where I expected to find a village and a life like the one we had had to leave behind in Sudan.

Part Three

REFUGE

John

braham and I were far from alone when we reached Pinyudu. The civil war in Sudan had touched millions of lives. Many had been killed on both sides. We were among the lucky ones who survived, although we did not feel lucky.

More than a quarter-million refugees from Sudan's civil war poured into Pinyudu and three other camps in Ethiopia in 1988. An even greater number probably died from human violence, animal attacks, hunger, thirst, and disease. Both Martha and I arrived in Pinyudu that year, but our paths didn't cross until much later.

Almost all of the survivors were male teenagers and boys as young as three or four. Older men had gone to war as soldiers or been killed in battle. Women and girls had been captured, killed, enslaved, or raped, leaving only a few hundred to reach Ethiopia.

At the time, the world paid little attention to the war and its victims because East Africa is so isolated and so seldom featured in the world's news. Eventually, news reporters from Europe and America began to learn about the refugees who had walked, like me, to safety and begun to scratch out a living in Ethiopia. They called us Lost Boys. They took the name from characters in the book *Peter Pan*.

News reporters called Pinyudu a "camp," but it was just a big, open place with no houses except a few belonging to the local Anyuak people. It had no fences, no running water, and no electricity. Everyone sat under trees or built shelters out of sticks. Abraham stayed with me for about two months and then went to live with other adults. I lived with boys who were mostly my age or somewhat younger. There were too many of us for adults to take care of, so the adults put some of the older boys like me in charge of the younger ones. At only thirteen years old, I became the supervisor of 1,200 boys. I made sure that sick boys got medical attention and oversaw the distribution of food.

We made our first huts without tools. I showed my group how to get wood from the forest outside camp without axes or saws. I climbed a tree until I got to the high branches. Then I grabbed a stout branch and jumped. As I fell, my weight bent the branch until it broke. Everyone watched and then copied me. That is how we got small logs for our hut. Then we pulled up grass in the camp and let it dry to make a roof.

We stayed hungry for many months. Once in a while we killed a crocodile in the river and ate it, but often we would go for days without food. Those were dark, difficult times.

Martha

For months Tabitha and I had lived in the wilds of Southern Sudan. All that while the elders in our group had told us that we were going to a new home where we would be safe and there would be lots of other Sudanese people who had had to run from their villages and who were homeless like us. At last the big day came. We got to Pinyudu.

But it wasn't a town, or even a village. It was nothing but a big open field. Standing and sitting and lying around that field were lots and lots and lots—hundreds, maybe a thousand—of us Sudanese. But there was no UN and no food. Like John and his group of Lost Boys, we went to bed hungry again, finding a place to lie down on the rocky red soil of Ethiopia to sleep. Tabitha was so skinny then that her bones poked up through her skin.

A few days after we got to Pinyudu, though, things changed. The UN's refugee agency had heard about all of us waiting in that field, and they arrived with dried corn, beans and lentils, oil, and salt. We were all so hungry that when we smelled the corn and lentils cooking, our bodies just couldn't wait. We started eating when the food was still hard, gobbling down the kernels and the lentils as fast as we could. Our stomachs couldn't take that hard food, and we just got sick. And the more we got sick, the more diseases spread.

John

The food the UN brought to Pinyudu was barely enough to live on. The group of children I lived with pooled our camp food rations and boiled them in a large metal cooking oil container we had cut in two to make a pot. We had no silverware, cups, or plates. Instead, we passed around a single bowl and each boy dipped into the food with his fingers. Often a boy would burn his hands and cry in pain. That led some of the boys to cut spoons out of scraps of metal so they could scoop their food without burning their fingers. Some boys found that if they carved really big spoons, they could get more food than the others. I thought that was unfair. One day when the boys went to the river to play, I took all of the spoons and destroyed them. That way we were all equal again.

The UN also brought us tools, blankets, and secondhand clothing. I got a shirt and wore it as proudly as anyone who ever wore fancy new clothes. On the pocket someone had stitched a strange, three-letter word. I could not read, so I got some of my friends to help say the word out loud. The letters read U-S-A. We pronounced it as one word, "Oosaw." I figured it must be a rich person who had plenty of clothes to give away.

I got a blanket too. It was a very important day when a boy got a blanket. The material was thick and warm, and it had a wonderful smell. When I got my UN blanket, I put it over my head and ran around camp, smelling it and saying, "This is mine." UN blankets had two sides and a layer of air in the middle. Some of the boys cut through the stitching along the edges and separated the blanket into two thinner sheets. They sold one sheet to a tribe of people who lived outside the camp in return for some monkey meat. Abraham bought a needle at a market and used it to sew my UN blanket into a new pair of shorts. Now I had something to wear with my new USA shirt.

Not long after we arrived, a terrible disease called cholera raced through the camp. It spreads wherever there is no clean water or sanitation. We had no latrines and no running water to wash ourselves, so everyone was filthy all the time. Flies flew everywhere. When we wanted drinking water, we took it from a stream next to our camp. We used that same stream to bathe, and from time to time we saw raw sewage in it that came from outside camp. We did not know about germs, but we were spreading them every day.

Cholera struck its victims suddenly. Boys who were too weak to walk to the usual places to relieve themselves just squatted in the middle of camp. They got so sick that their jaws clamped together and they could not talk. About one in five boys suffered from cholera on any particular day.

Sick boys gathered under the trees and called for their mothers and fathers. Every day, about one to three died in my group of 1,200. I organized gangs to carry the bodies outside camp for burial. This was before the UN brought us tools, so we had no shovels, axes, or spades. We dug into the earth with sharp sticks. We could only dig about eight to ten inches deep with our crude tools. We placed the bodies in these shallow graves, covered them with dirt, and went back to camp. Hyenas and lions dug up the graves at night to gnaw on the bodies. The hyenas woke me with their crazy laughter. When I visited the graves in the morning, an arm or leg stuck out of the ground. That happened all the time, until our adult caretakers showed us how to dig our latrines downstream from camp. Then the cholera slowly went away.

In addition to diseases, everyone in camp suffered from tuktuk. It is an African insect that burrows under the skin of the feet. There the insect feeds on blood and lays eggs. I was barefoot like everyone else, so I got tuktuk in my feet. It hurt so much I had trouble walking. Some boys' feet got so bad they could not walk at all. They just pushed themselves along the ground with their hands and arms, but that only led to tuktuk infesting their hands. Nothing did any good until we got kerosene from the UN. We washed our feet regularly in kerosene, and that worked for some people. The kerosene only seemed to make my feet swell up and sting. I got better by checking and cleaning my feet five or six times a day.

Some boys went insane from constant exposure to disease, starvation, and death. They refused to touch dead bodies. They cried out the names of loved ones. Some smeared their heads with filth and tried to get me to smell them. I tried to model good behavior and keep spirits up. I led some of the boys in singing hymns, and I always took my turn at burying the dead.

Some boys found clever ways to get enough to eat. We called one of the boys Ateermadang, which is the name of a spirit that the boy said dwelt inside him. The name roughly translates as *Problem Stopper*. The boy got food because he pretended to have special powers to see and know things others could not. Ateermadang offered his services to other boys. For a bowl of food with a tiny bit of meat, he would pretend to go into a trance and find lost objects and catch boys who had stolen things. He ate like a king for a while until someone exposed his lies. Ateermadang confessed everything. He said he had gone crazy with hunger and made up his stories just so someone would give him something to eat.

Martha

Though boys were put into their own groups with the older ones in charge, Sudanese elders, following our traditions, decided the girls needed to be looked after by adults. The elders advised the UN to put us with mothers of young children or with the few families that had made it to Pinyudu intact. Tabitha and I were lucky again because we were placed with a nice woman named Yar. She had three children of her own, and there were two other girls who were placed with her, so altogether she had seven children to take care of. The oldest one was her eight-year-old son. We all called her Mother, another Sudanese custom. That's what you call any woman your mother's age, as a sign of respect.

By this time the UN had given us little tents to sleep in, and we'd zip ourselves into them at night. After a while, the boys in the camp helped us build a small house. They made the walls with branches of trees and grass that they covered with mud, and the UN gave us a big piece of nylon fabric to use as a roof. I was so happy to have that little house as a home.

Yar was very good to us. After a while she began to raise chickens and a small vegetable garden in the little yard beside our house.

During the day we could almost feel carefree, like children again. We went swimming in the river, and we helped Yar with easy chores, such as sweeping our compound or collecting fire for cooking from a neighbor. In a Sudanese village, the first woman to start her cooking fire in the evening lets other people come to light small branches from her flame and carry them back to their yards to start their own fires.

I remember that at Pinyudu I could always hear the sound of pounding, as people pounded the dry corn kernels into meal to boil. They'd hollow a hole in a log and put the corn in there, then pound and grind it with a heavy stick. It was a lot of work. We'd eat boiled lentils with our corn, and sometimes Yar would trade the Anyuak a little of our UN oil for fish they'd caught in the river.

Once it grew dark, we went to sleep because the only light we had was from the cooking fires. You could see the dying embers from the fires as little sparks across the camp. Otherwise the only light was the moon staring down from the night sky.

The cooking oil cans John mentioned were useful in Yar's family, too. We cleaned the empty ones out and used them to collect water. Because I was one of the older children in Yar's "family," it was my chore to go to the river and draw water for cooking, drinking, and washing. People also washed clothes and other things in the river, so it was not exactly clean. I would try to wade out away from shore and dip the water there. I'd hoist the biggest can onto the top of my head or ask someone nearby to help me, and then carry a smaller can in my hand. The cans full of water were really heavy, and I had to stop to rest in the shade of trees on the way home. Someone from our house had to go to the river a few times a day to collect water. It was hard work, and after a while, it got scary.

At first we had loved swimming and splashing in the river. We'd even swim to the other side and sneak green mangoes off trees that belonged to the Anyuak. The unripe mangoes were sour, but we liked that taste. Then suddenly, people who went down to the river started to disappear, and we were sure crocodiles were lurking in the river and taking them. We stopped swimming and playing there, but we still had to wade in to fill our cans with water.

When we went to the river for water, we often saw the Anyuak people, and they fascinated us. They were probably of average height, but to us tall Dinka, they seemed like tiny, tiny people. They spoke a different language from ours, and at first we used hand signs to communicate, though after a while we picked up some of their language. More and more of them moved near camp. They don't keep cattle or grow gardens big enough to produce food to get them through the dry season. So when UN food bags would break open, leaving food behind, the

Anyuak would collect it. They also loved to trade us things we needed for the used T-shirts the UN gave us.

The UN workers tried to be fair in dividing up food and clothes among so many of us. They didn't want us to fight, so we had to get in line, and when our turn came, people handing out clothes would put their hands in a bag and pull out whatever they touched. One time I was lucky enough to get a dress. I was so, so, so happy that I had gotten this beautiful thing to wear. It was brown with short sleeves and a white and yellow collar, with a little bow under my chin. At first it was big on me, but over time it fit better. It was something I treasured, and I took good care of it. Little did I know that I would wear it for years.

At Pinyudu I met a girl named Nyayik, and we became good friends. We went to fetch water together, and we played with empty tuna and tomato paste cans, pretending to cook and be housewives. We would gather with other kids under this one particular tree to play. The boys in our group had something that looked like a fishing net, and they would put the net on the ground and then sprinkle it with broken corn to attract birds. The net had a long string on it, so the boys would move away from the net, but when a bird landed to eat the corn, they'd pull the string tight and catch the bird. When we had a few, we'd pluck them and boil them to eat.

On Sundays we'd all go to church together. Our church was made of mud—mud walls, mud benches—but we loved going there and singing and dancing and praying. We'd been taught exciting songs, songs of encouragement or sorrow.

Church was something we looked forward to, a happy thing. It was in Pinyudu that I took the name Martha. I wanted a name from the Bible, and also Martha was the name of an old neighbor. I liked the way it sounded with my Dinka name, Arual. We all tried to choose a name that would sound good with our Dinka name, or rhyme with it.

The UN had started schools in Pinyudu, and some of the boys went. But the Dinka didn't believe that girls and boys were meant to do the same kind of things and there was no encouragement for us girls to go to school, even though the UN people kept telling us about the importance of education.

The first white people I ever saw were those UN people at Pinyudu. They were Europeans, and they seemed so odd to us with their long noses and white skin. The men were much fatter than our Dinka men, and the hot weather was really hard on them. They wore these shirts that did not cover them up, and we could see hair, lots of hair, on their bodies, and sweat. This was so different from our own bodies. We would just look at them, stare at them, marveling.

When the rains came to Pinyudu, we stayed inside most of the time. It rained so hard that the little creeks filled with water, and the river would be full of fallen trees. We got our water then from seasonal ponds. We'd get rained on going to get it and be soaking wet and cold after that. We didn't have any towels, so we just dried ourselves with our dirty clothes as best we could.

Still, I liked the rainy season. It was a time to rest and stay inside and tell stories to each other. A lot of the stories were about animals and being brave around animals, or things like why hyena is called hyena or why an animal acts the way it does. But some were sad human stories, like what can happen to you when your parents are not there.

Every time we heard that new people were arriving in Pinyudu, a lot of us Lost Children would go and wait for them, looking at every adult arriving and hoping that our mother and father might be among them. We had been told that people had been scattered when the fighting started in Southern Sudan, so we kept hoping that our parents were still alive, that one day they would make it to Pinyudu. And every time they weren't in the new group, we would leave heartbroken. Even though our little group at Yar's home had started to feel like a family, a safe place, it couldn't fill the hole in my heart left by my missing parents.

We didn't have radios or TVs at Pinyudu, so when the UN wanted to tell us something, they'd send a couple of guys around with megaphones to spread the word. Usually the guys with the megaphones would just be reminding us that we had to come and re-register ourselves with the camp officials, something we had to do every couple of months. But one day, after we'd been at the camp for about three years, we heard the megaphones, and it wasn't the usual thing. What the man was shouting into the megaphones was shocking. He kept saying, "Tonight we are going to leave" over and over. "You have to pack your belongings and get ready to leave."

John

Slowly I had come to like the life of a Lost Boy in Pinyudu. We shared our daily chores. We played and swam and even started to dance and sing. But good times never last forever. Ethiopia was in the middle of its own civil war. In May 1991, when I was sixteen years old, the rebels drove the president out of the country and set up a new government that was friendly with Northern Sudan. The new government decided to close the refugee camps. We had to pack and leave Pinyudu. We didn't even have time to harvest the corn and vegetables we had planted near our huts.

The adults in camp who acted as our caretakers had a long discussion among themselves and decided to head back into Sudan. We learned we would go toward the town of Pochala, which the southern forces still held. There was not much else we could do.

Part Four

WAR

Martha

We couldn't believe it! It was all happening so fast, and everything was suddenly in confusion as people gathered their few small belongings. We put what we could in the nylon bags that corn and lentils had come in. If people had known ahead of time, they would have ground corn to prepare for the trip, but there was no time. Some people killed their chickens and ate them quickly.

That night there was silence all over the camp, from our little homes to the Lost Boys' compounds. The UN wanted to keep the news of our leaving from the Anyuak, because they were afraid the Anyuak might take things from us by force. At first we had all gotten along with the Anyuak, but tensions had grown and there had been a few fights with them. Still, some of the older Dinka boys had married Anyuak girls, and they were staying behind.

I remember it was bedtime and dark as we left our new home. We were tired, but being scared kept us wide awake. We walked through the forest single file, a long, long line of children broken here and there by the figure of an adult. Tabitha was six now, old enough now to know that something was happening. She had forgotten about the trip to Pinyudu, I think, and how bad it was, but I remembered, and walking again brought back the memories of that long, hard walk to Ethiopia just three years before.

We had to walk all night to leave the Pinyudu area. We rested during the day under the trees, and by the next day we made it to the Gilo River. The UN had food waiting for us there because there were only a few boats to take us across the river, and it would take many days to get all of us ferried over to the Sudanese side.

People settled in beside the Gilo, relaxing and cooking and visiting together. In the mornings we'd get in line for a boat, but by day's end, we'd still be waiting. So the next day we'd get back in the line again. The man who was organizing the boats happened to be Yar's cousin, and finally she explained to him that, with all us kids, it was going to take her a long time to walk to Pochala. She asked him if we could get on a boat sooner, and he said okay.

As we stepped into the little boat, the river looked big with a rough current, and the people on the other side looked small and far away. But we made it safely across and spent the night on the riverbank there. In the morning we joined a bigger group and started walking again.

John

I must have reached the Gilo River after Martha had already crossed, because my crossing was as different from hers as night is from day. I was resting and eating my lunch on the side of the river when the Ethiopian army attacked us with bullets, mortar shells, and grenades. People jumped into the water and began to swim toward the other side.

I leaped up, scattering corn meal. Bullets zipped through the air, making birdlike sounds as they went by my head.

I ran toward the Gilo River. I was not a good swimmer, so I hesitated and looked for the best place to cross. More bullets whizzed by my head, and more grenades landed around me. I panicked and jumped in the water, flopping into the mud and reeds at the river's edge. The impact knocked the air out of my lungs. I struggled into the muddy water and began to kick toward the far side.

A big man from the Nuba tribe grabbed me. He was panicking too, and he could not swim at all. He pushed down on me to try to keep his own head above the water.

"*Sa'adni! Sa'adni!*" he yelled in Arabic. "Help me, help me!"

I had learned a little Arabic in Pinyudu, where it was used as the common language to communicate among all of the tribes. "I can't help you," I shouted at the big man. I kept struggling and swimming and kicking. The Nuba let go. I do not know what happened to him. I surfaced, free from his grasp, and started swimming again toward the far shore.

At home in Duk Payuel, I had learned how to swim on my back, but I had never learned the crawl very well. So when I surfaced, I flipped face up and started to do the backstroke, staring up at the sky. As I slowly made progress, I glanced anxiously left and right. Everywhere, people were screaming and flailing. Bullets and shrapnel hit their bodies and put blood in the water. I knew crocodiles must be in the river and that they could smell blood. I did not see any crocodiles near me, thank goodness.

Some of the adult caretakers from Pinyudu had managed to string a rope across the river, and boys who couldn't swim were pulling themselves across. Others were crossing in the small boats belonging to the Anyuak tribesmen, who used them to fish on the river. At least one boat overturned in the middle of the river, dumping four Lost Boys into the water. A crocodile killed one, and two of the other three drowned.

Another boy found me in the water. He tried to grab me to keep from drowning. "If you hold me like that I can't push water. I can't carry you," I screamed. He relaxed just a bit. I held his arm with one hand and began paddling with my other hand. After a few strokes, I switched hands and kept going. We slowly made our way across until I could feel mud under my feet.

The boy I had dragged across the river scrambled up the bank, and I followed on my hands and knees. At the top, I turned and looked at the shore where I had started. Smoke and dust filled the air, and shells exploded on the ground. Boys were running for their lives all around me. Some fell as bullets fired from the far shore tore into their bodies. I ran too, until I was out of range of the guns and mortars. Fortunately for us, the Ethiopian army would not cross a crocodile-infested river. We ran and then walked until we felt safe.

I still have bad dreams about crossing the Gilo River. I still wonder what war does to people to make them shoot unarmed children. Do those Ethiopian soldiers ever get nightmares? I do not know.

Of the roughly 20,000 Sudanese who went into the Gilo River, maybe 2,000 to 3,000 died in the attempt to get across. Those who survived found themselves back in Sudan, where the war raged on and food was still scarce. Once again I had no food or shelter and no immediate way to get any. It was obvious my long ordeal was far from over.

Martha

We'd been walking about a day and a half and we were almost halfway to Pochala when we heard the booming of big guns. We didn't know what was going on, so we kept walking. We were more concerned about lions than guns then, because someone had seen a lion. We were told not to make any noise. We felt like we were going to be attacked by a lion at any minute. At night, we slept on the road, but when I tried to sleep, the crack of a tree in the forest or the wind blowing or the grass swaying made me think that something deadly was about to come out of the forest. Lions aren't afraid of a big group. They'll go right into that group and grab someone. It's just a matter of whether it's your day to be grabbed. This wasn't my day, or Tabitha's. And after a few days of walking, we came to Pochala, another place to start over.

John

I walked away from the death and destruction of the Gilo River. Others walked too, including Abraham. He had survived, and he helped gather the refugees from Pinyudu and take care of them. As the Lost Boys found one another, we came together in groups and marveled that we still lived. One man had avoided the bullets and mortar shells but not the animals in the river. While swimming across, he lost a hand and part of an arm to the jaws of a hungry crocodile. We called him Mkono Moja, which means "One Hand Man" in Kiswahili. Considering the fate of so many who had died in the Gilo, he was fortunate.

For a while, I hoped that I might return to my village of Duk Payuel and look for my family. But as I thought about my situation, I realized I could not go back. Civil war still raged in Sudan. The northern armies controlled much of the homeland of the Dinka. And there could be no life and no peace in Southern Sudan for anyone with dark skin who opposed the national government.

So I set out with the other refugees for the Sudanese town of Pochala, not far from the Ethiopian border. SPLA soldiers from Southern Sudan, our friends, had taken the town in battle but did not know how long they could hold it. I hoped to stay there as long as it was safe. Then, if I had to, I would move on to keep away from the invading army. Thousands of other boys from Pinyudu joined me on the trek to Pochala. We went along a muddy road in a single line. We went slowly, as we had no food or water and were all on foot. Our line stretched out so far between the first boy and the last that it took two days for everyone to pass the same spot.

There wasn't much to Pochala. The battle for the town had left it in ruins. I spent my first night in an abandoned military barracks. There was almost no food in the town. SPLA soldiers came and gave us something to eat from time to time, but mostly we Lost Boys stayed hungry. Over the next few months, our numbers swelled as refugees poured in from other Sudanese towns. The soldiers just didn't have enough food to share with so many.

Martha

In Pochala, just as in our first days in Pinyudu, we used the trees for shelter. We survived on the small bit of food that Yar had managed to take away with her from Pinyudu—a little dried corn and lentils. In a few days it was gone.

Still we were so lucky that we had survived. Our hearts were filled with pain because now we knew why we had heard booming guns on our walk here. When the news came of the killing at the Gilo River, everybody cried and cried, not just us children. So many people we had known in Pinyudu were gone, shot down there or carried away by crocodiles or the river. And we kept thinking, "The next time danger comes, it will be my turn to go." That thought and the loss of our friends and relatives at the Gilo haunted us. It was another darkness we had to live with. We felt hopeless.

We began to trade the few clothes we had brought with us to the Anyuak for food. They would come to town and bring corn and millet, sorghum, and beans and take the T-shirts or other clothes the UN had given us in exchange. Maybe a T-shirt would be worth two cups of maize. Some people sold all the clothes they had and were left naked and starving. I still had the brown dress that I had been so happy to get in Pinyudu. It was the only thing I had left to wear. Now, it was torn and dirty, but I kept patching it.

Some people were dying, but others were saying, "The UN is coming, the UN is coming." The problem was that there was nowhere at Pochala for planes with food and supplies to land, no landing strip. For three weeks after we ran out of things to trade to the Anyuak, there was no food.

When you don't have anything to eat, you just think about eating. Your stomach grumbles, and then it hurts, pinching, and you have no energy. When you're really starving, your stomach hurts until you don't want to do anything. It feels like your whole body is shutting down. That's how I felt when I finally heard the plane overhead.

At first we were afraid the plane had been sent by the northern Sudanese to bomb us, and people hid wherever they could. But some elders had been told that planes were coming with food. When they told us this, people started running toward the sound of the plane, and in a few minutes it was dropping what looked like paper toward us. But as the "paper" got closer, we could see that it was really sacks of corn and beans. Some sacks split open when they hit the ground, and corn and beans spilled everywhere. People were taking what they could from the ground. They didn't care if the food was mixed with dust and debris. This was food, and they were starving.

Yar came home with some dried beans and corn and sorghum. She called us to come and separate the food from the dirt and dried leaves and grass. It took us a long time to do that, but we were happy because we knew we would eat at last.

Yar ground some of the corn into a powder, and that day we had a meal. The following morning the elders distributed more food. They handed it out a little bit at a time, to make sure everyone got some. Every few days after that the UN would make another drop. But they couldn't drop oil or salt, things that would have given the food some taste, so the food had almost no flavor at all.

For about a month we stayed under trees. It was the rainy season and we were wet all the time, with no dry clothes to change into. After a while some Lost Boys built us a simple shelter made of tall grass and leafy tree branches. We had to be very careful not to light any fire close to it, because it would have burst into flames.

Almost overnight Pochala became a big town, full of refugees. I was so happy when I found that my good friend Nyayik had made it to Pochala, and we started spending lots of time together. We went to an outdoor church under a tree that had logs for seats. It felt like things were starting to calm down and that we had made a new life, yet again. Over the simple shelter we lived in, we now had a nylon tarp for a roof, supplied by the UN. But that wasn't enough to protect us from what came next.

John

One day, I heard the sound of an airplane. I hoped it might be a plane from the UN bringing us food. Instead, as I listened closely, the sound became clear. It was the engine of a bomber from the northern armies. It flew over our refugee camp and dropped its load of bombs— *boom! boom! boom!* Fountains of dirt flew into the air where the bombs struck the earth. A couple of boys were injured. After that raid, everyone all over town started digging trenches. Whenever we heard a bomber overhead, we dived into our safe holes in the ground.

Thank goodness the UN and the Red Cross kept up their relief missions, flying over Pochala and dropping loads of food, medicine, and clothes. They even dropped fish hooks so we could catch our dinner in the rivers nearby. We cleared some ground for a landing strip, and then the planes began landing to make their deliveries. We got very good at listening for the sound of airplane engines and distinguishing the sounds of enemy bombers from friendly cargo transports.

Gradually in early 1992, I noticed the bombers coming more often. The northern armies were on the move. They advanced toward Pochala and captured many southern towns, leaving tens of thousands of Sudanese homeless. Now even more people were like us—refugees on the move.

One day our adult caretakers, including Abraham, decided that it would be unsafe to linger in Pochala. The northern armies were closing in. The caretakers stayed up into the evening and discussed our future. They decided we must walk farther into the interior, toward the border with Kenya. The journey would take us through jungles, grasslands, and desert. But it was the best chance we had for survival.

Martha

Again we started packing. We had only been in Pochala a few months, but we had to leave, this time heading for Kapoeta, a large town near the border with Kenya that the SPLA also controlled. We weren't sure if we would run into the militia, so once again we had to sneak away. For a very intense day and night we walked silently.

Soon we were in the territory of tribes I had never seen. Some had made scars on their bodies as a sign of beauty. Lots of people in Southern Sudan do that, but some of the married women here had stretched their bottom lips by piercing and weighting them, and the men had done the same things with their ears. We had never seen such long, long lips and ears before. What we ate, we got from trading with these local tribes. Some of them had no problem with us; some attacked us. One tribe even tricked us by first trading goats to us for some empty cooking oil cans we had, then sneaking up on us to steal their goats back. There was shooting, and some of my group was killed. It seemed that I was going to live around shooting and violence all my life.

I was traveling with hundreds of people all walking at all different speeds. Yar and we children were usually in the slow group. Tabitha was big enough now to walk on her own, but she was scared and crying a lot. Sometimes when it was time to move on again, she would say she didn't want to keep going.

John

So began what turned into a 500-mile journey. We walked from village to village. The towns had names such as Raat, Buma, Kapoeta, and Nairus. We kept moving farther south to get away from the fighting. We eventually realized that if we ran out of safe land in Sudan we would have to go into the neighboring country of Kenya. At the end of the line was Kapoeta then Lokichokio, just over the border. If we made it that far, the pursuing armies would not follow us.

As one of the eldest of the boys in my group, I acted as a leader on the march to Kapoeta. I told the younger boys what to do and helped care for them. As we marched, we sang songs. There were Christian songs and proud songs about what it means to be a Southern Sudanese. We made up many songs on the spot. Some were funny. Some reminded us of our homes and our families, and they were sad. Some just helped us march in rhythm. One boy sang out, "I am malaria!" That meant he felt very strong because malaria can hurt anyone.

We all felt proud because we were walking a route of our own choosing, and not at the point of any gun.

At a town called Pakok we found some yams and peanuts. That filled our bellies for a while. But further south the sun rose higher and hotter, and we ran out of food and water. One night the group of boys I was marching with pooled the last of our beans and water. We ate those, and then we had no more food.

The next day was over 100 degrees. The ground was so hot that blisters formed and burst on the bottoms of my bare feet and the dry air made me very thirsty. I tried to keep going, but finally I had to stop. I lay down and fell asleep right next to the road, right in the middle of the day. All around me, other boys did the same. We were too thirsty and hungry to keep going, and too tired to care. I thought I would die.

As if by a miracle, a UN truck arrived that day to bring water to the line of Lost Boys. I ducked my head in the truck's water tank and took a big gulp. It tasted wonderful. I found the strength to keep moving.

From that day onward, UN truck drivers visited our line of refugees every day. They brought water and food. They also brought news of the outside world. They said the northern armies were not far behind us and that we must keep moving. From a caretaker who had a radio, we also learned that news reporters from the outside world had begun to take notice of the Lost Boys. A radio network in England called the BBC was reporting on our movements.

We came to the outskirts of Kapoeta in the barren, dusty land called the Tingilic Desert. A native tribe called the

Taposa lived in the desert and envied the food that we carried. At first, the Taposa tribesmen collected any leftover food we discarded whenever the UN trucks arrived with a new supply. Then they began attacking the boys at the back of the line to steal their food right after they got it. I was walking with my group of boys when the Taposa attacked.

Being attacked was frightening to begin with, and in this case the timing couldn't have been worse. One of the boys in my group had eaten some undercooked beans that had made his stomach swell with gas. His belly grew so large that he felt terribly sick and could barely move his arms and legs. I tried to help him by making him drink soapy water to make the swelling go down, but it did no good. He just lay in a grove of thorny trees in too much pain to move. And that's when the Taposa attacked.

Tribesmen came on fast, firing their guns in the air. At first, they fired to let their fellow tribesmen know when to start the attack, and to scare us so we would drop our food. As they kept on firing, some shot directly at the Lost Boys. I tried to get everyone in my group to run, but the boy with the big belly could not move. I hit his belly with a stick, trying to force him to his feet. He just cried.

"This is the end of my life! I'm going to die," he whimpered.

"Stop!" I screamed at him. "Get up. We have to go."

I couldn't just leave him there. With the help of a couple of other boys, I tried to roll him like a ball along the trail, but that was no good. Finally, we made a stretcher out of some wooden poles and a blanket, and we carried the round-belly boy. The Taposa followed us and fired their guns again. Fortunately, a UN car came along and scared the Taposa away. One of the men in the car got out and gave the round boy some medicine. I think they took him in the car with them. When I got to Kapoeta, I found the boy. The swelling in his belly had gone down a bit, and he felt much better. We called him The Boy Who Ate Beans, but as far as I know he never ate beans again.

We stayed in Kapoeta for only three days. Like the other towns we had passed through, it soon fell to the invading soldiers.

Martha

We knew we needed to keep moving toward Kenya, but we were afraid of the local tribes between Kapoeta and the Kenyan border. A safe way to get there was in one of the big tractor-trailer trucks that carried cargo from Kenya into Sudan. When they headed back to Kenya, they were empty, their cargoes already delivered. But many of the drivers of these trucks were cruel. They would pretend they were stopping for the refugees, and the refugees would run toward them, then the drivers would suddenly take off before the refugees got to their trucks. Then they would stop again a little farther down the road, and the refugees would run toward them again. In this way, the cruel drivers led people farther and farther from the safety of Kapoeta, into the countryside where they could be attacked by hostile tribes.

Yar was smart enough not to let us run after those teasing drivers. She had another plan. On the way to Kapoeta, she had traded something—I don't know what—to one of the local tribes for a big chicken. Now people from Kenya like to eat chicken very much, so she traded that chicken to a Kenyan driver in exchange for a ride for all of us. We got into the big, empty tractor-trailer truck and sat down and watched as the dry desert land just rolled away behind us. So fast, so painless, not like walking step by step by step to get where you want to go. It was my first time in a vehicle since I had been separated from my parents four years before. At last we were headed for safety.

Part Five

REFUGE

John

We kept walking and walking. One day, we crossed the Kenyan border without realizing it. There was nothing to mark that we had entered a new country. Our spirits rose as we realized the soldiers would not follow us. We walked into the town of Lokichokio. There we stayed for two months until we received news from the UN. There were too many boys to stay in that one town. The UN High Commissioner for Refugees had decided to relocate all of us to a new camp sixty miles inside northwestern Kenya. The camp would form around the tiny town of Kakuma in the high, windswept desert.

The UN sent open-topped trucks to Lokichokio to take us to Kakuma. The truck beds were covered with benches for us to sit on. I had never ridden in a car or truck before. I got aboard the truck carrying a bundle of sticks. I had made a crude hut out of the sticks in Lokichokio and wanted to take them with me to Kakuma. Lots of other boys on the truck had their own bundles of sticks. I put a mark on my bundle to show it was mine. The truck bounced and jolted us along some very bad roads, but we arrived safely at Kakuma.

It did not look like much. The campsite was barren and dusty. Every day the temperature soared toward 100 degrees Fahrenheit or more, and dry winds blanketed the camp with a fine, red dust that covered the ground like snow. Swirling clouds of dust blocked out the sun. Cars had to drive with their headlights on just to make it across camp. The first time I tried to walk through the dust, I sank into it up to my knees. I was a red-black man.

Kakuma was an end and a beginning. It was the end of our wandering. The Kenyan government ordered that all refugees stay in camps such as Kakuma. We could not leave it to go look for work or to try to find a new life in one of Kenya's cities. Instead, we knew we would be stuck there for quite some time. But Kakuma also held out hope that our lives might change for the better. Here at last we would have freedom from fear. We would get food from the UN. We would have access to schools. We would build circles of friends and make new families. And we would work hard to try to make a brighter future for ourselves and, we hoped, our fellow Sudanese.

A typical Dinka village in Southern Sudan, similar to John's village of Duk Payuel

A young Dinka boy milks a cow near his home in Sudan. With their long horns and slender bodies, cows in this part of the world look very different from the dairy cows many people in North America and Europe are used to seeing.

Here, more than 3,000 lost children arrive from a refugee camp in Ethiopia back to Sudan after walking hundreds of miles without sufficient food or wate

A group of Lost Boys gather to listen to caretakers at the Pinyudu camp in February 1989. John is somewhere in the back of the group.

AFRICA
Khartoum
SUDAN
Area
Enlarged
UGANDA
Nairobi
KENYA
ETHIOPIA

kilometers 100
miles 100

Jokau Gambela Dembi
Dolo

Akobo *Gilo* ETHIOPIA
Pinyudu
Duk Payuel Pochala
Likwangoli Yeki
Akelo
Pibor Post
Sudd Swamp S U D A N *Kangen*
Mountain Nile
Bor *Kenamuke
Swamp*

*Kobowen
Swamp*

Juba Kapoeta *Lotagipi
Swamp*
Lolimi
Lokichokio
K E N Y A
Kakuma
Moyo Kaabong
Albert Nile Atiak Rhino
Camp
U G A N D A Kotido
Gulu
Pakwach

······ John's route   ······ Martha's route   ······ Combined route   —— Road

Martha (standing, left)
with her friends at the
Kakuma Refugee Camp
in Kenya in 1998

John (second from the right) and his
friends drink porridge after school in
Kakuma in 1999.

John and Martha walk out of the church after their American wedding ceremony on June 2, 2007.

Martha and John with their children: daughter Agot and son Leek. They welcomed a third child, a daughter named Akur, in May 2010.

Martha

It seemed that the trees were always our first home. And that's the way it was in Kakuma. There were no real shelters, so we crowded under the trees. But the trees couldn't protect us from the wind. The wind would pick up red dust and sand and hurl it at us in great gusts. Everyone had dust on their faces, in their hair, in their noses. If you sneezed, you sneezed dust. If you coughed, you coughed dust.

Still, we were lucky because it rained a little when we first came to Kakuma and that settled the dust. We didn't know it then, but it never rained in that part of Kenya. The local tribe, the Turkana, were amazed to see rain. They said that God really must be with the Dinka if it rained on us.

The Turkana themselves had no food and no jobs. They had been dying of disease and starvation, and the few goats they kept had been dying as well. But when we started to arrive, their lives got better because the UN was there with food. The Turkana would come to the camp, and we would share food, whatever we had, with them. We knew what it was like to be hungry and desperate. Later on, when Kakuma was well established, the Turkana gathered firewood in the forests to trade with us for corn or clothes. That way, they could eat, too.

Our leaders at Kakuma told the UN that we should be divided into groups according to our clans and the counties we were from in Sudan. The boys were grouped that way and lived together. The Lost Girls were all placed with families. Tabitha and I got to stay with Yar, and after a while her husband's brother Deng came to stay with us. He had gone to Uganda when he had had to flee Southern Sudan, then he had heard that Yar was at Kakuma, so he came there to be with her. Neither of them had spouses anymore, so they became a couple. That is a Dinka custom, for a widowed woman to live with her brother-in-law. And Dinka men always have more than one wife.

Life in Kakuma followed the same patterns at first as life had in Pinyudu and Pochala. We got help from the Lost Boys to build a small house, and when the UN started bringing cooking oil to us in big metal cans, people cut up the empty cans and fit the pieces together to make a metal roof. We planted a garden, so we had fresh vegetables to eat, including cabbage, something I had never eaten before. I thought it was delicious.

The UN dug wells for water, but getting it was an ordeal. We girls took turns waking up really early in the morning, before the sun had risen, to get in the long line at the well. Then we'd carry our full cans home.

John

If I had grown to adulthood in a Dinka village like my brothers and sisters before me, I would have had many relatives and many traditions to guide me along the way. Dinka children learn respect from their parents and other elders, who are quick with discipline and encouragement. They learn the value of education by absorbing the laws and traditions of the tribe. They learn responsibility through taking care of goats and cattle. And they are tested again and again until they learn courage and leadership.

I regret that I never had the chance to be initiated into manhood in the Dinka way. Dinka boys of fifteen or sixteen must go through an intense ritual of initiation. They live totally isolated for about two months. They fend for themselves and kill and cook their own food. When their time is up, they return to their villages not as boys but as men. That means they can fight lions, go to war, and have all of the privileges of adulthood except marriage, which Dinka men traditionally put off until they are about age thirty. People of my father's generation sometimes showed off having passed through the initiation by carving scars into their foreheads and removing their lower teeth, but that tradition has almost disappeared. None of this happened to me because I was only thirteen when I had to flee Duk Payuel and seventeen when I arrived in Kakuma. I had spent my initiation time on the run. To this day, some Sudanese jokingly refer to me as a "boy" because I never went through the initiation into adulthood.

We Lost Boys had to raise ourselves and each other in Kakuma. Imagine thousands of children and teenagers all in one place, with only a handful of adults. Does that sound like a playground? Or a paradise? I assure you it was neither.

We had our fun and our playtime, of course. We played soccer and alueth, and we wrestled and told stories in the Dinka way. After a while we teenagers even started dancing on Saturday nights. We invited some of the Lost Girls to dance with us, but there were never enough of them for every boy to have a dance partner.

These were the highlights of camp life. But of course life at Kakuma wasn't all fun. The biggest problems were food and shelter. We refugees divided ourselves into circles of a dozen or so. We said we belonged to a "group," but really each group acted like a family. We built a shelter out of tree limbs, palm branches, and whatever other materials we could find, but the huts leaked when it rained and always needed repairs. Food was scarce, but we shared what we had with other members of the group.

About every sixteen days, UN trucks arrived in Kakuma

to distribute dry food. Every boy got six kilograms, or about thirteen pounds, during each visit. Mostly we received corn, wheat flour, and lentils. That had to last us more than two weeks until the trucks came again. Some of the boys in my group had a little money from selling their rations or the vegetables they grew to others in camp or to the native Kenyans. We used the money to buy sugar and salt to help flavor our meals.

We pooled our food rations and ate them sparingly to make them last. I was in charge of dinner for our group. I insisted that we eat only one meal a day. I asked the group when they wanted to eat. We settled on 10 a.m. and set up a schedule so that each boy would get a turn at being the cook. I measured out one day's worth of corn meal every morning and gave it to the chef of the day. He dropped it in a kettle of boiling water and then added a bit of sugar and salt. When the corn meal turned into a watery yellow porridge, it was time for dinner. Every boy dipped his cup into the porridge and drank. That was all we had to eat for twenty-four hours.

No matter how much we tried to ration the food, we always seemed to run out before the UN trucks came again. We might go a day or two without any food. If the trucks got delayed by bad roads or bad weather, it might be a couple more days before we got anything to eat. We called these times without food our "black days." Kakuma was pitch black at night on those days because nobody bothered to kindle a cooking fire.

To make the time pass until the next shipment of food arrived, we told stories and played games. We tried to trick our bellies into thinking we were full by drinking a lot of water. But that only worked for a while, and then our hunger pains would come back. When we couldn't avoid the subject of food any longer, I would remind the boys in my group of an old Dinka saying: "Hunger does not know *nguik*." The nguik is the spot on a cow's neck where you stab it with a spear to kill it. Hunger did not know how to find that spot on a human being. What I meant was that hunger might make us feel bad for a few days, but it would not kill us. I used that saying to remind everyone to be strong, like a Dinka.

When the youngest boys got very hungry, some of the older boys played a trick to help them. They went to the clinic and pretended to have very bad diarrhea. The treatment for diarrhea is to drink water mixed with powders containing sugar, salt, and medicine. The pretenders got packets of the powder at the clinic and returned to the group to share. We all drank the medicine. It gave us strength to get through another day. I feel a little bad about the trick now, not knowing if some boys who were really sick couldn't get that medicine because we had gotten it first.

Every year, each boy received a ration card. When caretakers doled out the food, they trimmed a boy's ration card and pressed his finger in invisible ink. Some boys stole ration cards and tried to go through the food line twice. However, they were swiftly caught. The caretakers made them put their fingers under a special kind of light. It made the invisible ink glow blue or purple. The caretakers took their cards away, and the Kenyan police put them in jail.

With only a few adults to supervise us, we had to create our own ways of living from day to day. We could have given up on going to church and school, but we did not. Church and school are important to the Dinka. Children embrace them even when there are no adults around. At Kakuma, church helped give us hope that better things would come our way. School helped give us the tools to change our lives.

Every night, children gathered to sing and worship God. My church group was No. 36, and it had 600 to 800 boys. For two hours, from 6 p.m. to 8 p.m., we met outdoors for church. Only we didn't call it church. We called it "synagogue," and we modeled it on the Jews of the Old Testament. We were Christians, but we were mimicking the ways of the Israelites when they wandered in the desert without a home. I was the one who supervised the services. I kept track of who would give the sermon each night, and I made sure the worshipers had tambourines and drums. Boys who wanted to preach came to me for tryouts. Those who made the cut prepared themselves in the Dinka way. They isolated themselves and fasted for a while. Going without food wasn't too hard when there was so little to go around in the first place.

I also started school at the refugee camp. There had been no formal schools in Duk Payuel, so I was very excited to begin the first grade. I was eighteen years old when I had my first school lesson.

Everybody started school at the same time—big kids and small kids, Dinka and Nuer and members of all of the other tribes. We learned in groups of sixty. I remember my first day of class very clearly. I sat with my group in the powdery red dust of Kakuma in the shade of an achuil tree and nervously waited for the teacher. We had no blackboard or chalk or desks or chairs or pencils or paper. All we had was an easel made out of sticks and nails, topped with a sheet of cardboard. For chalk, we had lumps of charcoal from the cooking pits.

I remember my teacher's name: Atak. He was Sudanese and spoke Dinka. He walked through our circle of sitting boys and gave us our first lesson.

"Good morning, pupils. I am your teacher, Atak," he said in Dinka. "When I say 'Good morning, pupils,' you say, 'Good morning, teacher' to me. Let's try it."

"Good morning, pupils!"

"Good morning, teacher!"

"This is our first lesson. It is about respect," Atak said.

We felt right at home. Respect is the first thing a child learns in a Dinka family—respect for mother, father, aunts, uncles, other children, and animals. Every adult must be given great dignity. Children must do what an adult says to do, whether it is a parent or someone else from the village. What they say about African communities is true: It takes a village to raise a child.

With Atak as our teacher, we learned to say "thank you" and "good morning" and many other words and phrases. After Atak was satisfied with our manners, he took roll by asking us to stand and say our names. "My name is John Bul Dau," I said, and Atak wrote that in his register. Atak said he would read us the roll again and asked us to respond with a new word. It was in a new language, called English, he said. He gave us the word and we all practiced it. It was the first English word I knew. So, when Atak called my name, I responded as he told me: "Yes!" I was very excited.

Next we learned our ABCs. We had nothing to write on except the red dust at our feet, so that is what we used. I drew the letter "A" with my finger. That night, my first homework assignment was to practice drawing that letter. I had seen that letter before, on my shirt at Pinyudu that said "USA." Now I was on the brink of learning all of the letters and how to put them together to form words.

My group went home and practiced our letter "A." Every day we learned new letters and new numbers. Then we learned new words and how to make sentences. We practiced in our huts, where every night a new boy would be chosen to play teacher and lead the lesson, while everyone else played their parts as students. Slowly, we taught ourselves to read, write, and speak English, and to do math. I started reading everything I could find that had English words. I read the ingredients on food packages and the words on T-shirts. I read the sides of vegetable oil cans. It was a big, big day when I got my first book and Atak began to introduce me to the world outside East Africa. Some books had pictures of cities in faraway places. Some had pictures and words that seemed totally strange. They showed things like coffee pots, microwave ovens, and kitchen sinks. I had seen nothing like them. Our camp had no electricity and no running water. What did I know of computers and television sets and other items of daily life in big cities?

Sometimes the teachers knew as little as the pupils. Once we read a book about some Kenyan children. They tried to stay awake one night but fell asleep when clouds covered the moon. One of the pupils asked about the English word "cloud," which was new to our vocabulary. The teacher did not know but pretended that he did. He said a cloud was a very big bird. Later I learned the truth. I smile when I think of that teacher.

I worked hard at my lessons. I progressed very quickly through school until I reached the equivalent of middle school. I had to study many subjects and get passing grades to get to the equivalent of high school. It was very hard because we were in Kenya so the exams were in Kiswahili, a third language I had to master beyond Dinka and English. I studied in the evening until the sun set, and I stood in line to use the little libraries that missionaries had built for us. Thankfully, I managed to pass.

Then came high school lessons. I felt as if my life depended on my passing the exam that would give me a high school diploma. Again I studied very hard. The libraries were afraid their books would get stolen, so none of the books could be checked out. I sat on the library floor and hand-copied books on history, geography, civics, agriculture, and other subjects. Then I took those papers home and studied them. Just as before, I worked with other boys in my group to play teacher and students. We drilled each other every day from sunrise to sunset. I encouraged everyone to start studying early in the morning.

"Get up! Get up! Time to study!" I shouted at 4 a.m. I also

walked around beating a piece of tin with a stick. *Bang! Bang!* That is how we started our school day.

Finally the big day came. I took the test and passed with a C-plus. It was a very hard test. I was very proud. Earning a high school diploma in East Africa marks a man as smart and successful. I dreamed of being a teacher, a politician, or someone who ran a large organization.

Everyone celebrated earning their diplomas with music and dancing. We rented a tape player and some Congolese dance music tapes, and we had a party. Some of the Lost Girls came to the party and danced with us.

Seeing girls made me think of families. I had lived in Kakuma for several years and was no longer a boy. Some of the Lost Boys and Lost Girls had gotten married and begun to raise families. Nobody knew how long we would have to stay in camp. Perhaps the camps would last until the war ended in Sudan, and nobody knew how long that would be. But I was in no hurry to marry. I knew I would need to provide for a wife and children, and I was a long way from having a job and a home of my own.

Martha

UN schools were open to girls just as in Pinyudu, and now that we were older, we sometimes managed to attend. But if we weren't finished with our morning chores by the time school started at nine, we weren't allowed to go. The families we Lost Girls were staying with didn't encourage us to go to school anyway. They would rather have us stay at home and work for them. And besides, an education wasn't something a Dinka girl had been taught to value. It didn't mean anything to us. We would say to ourselves, "Oh, maybe I will go to school tomorrow," but then the next day, after we'd fetched water and swept our compound and ground maize, it was too late to go and we were already tired.

Gradually, though, by going to classes now and then, I began to understand English. Learning a new language made me really excited about learning more. And in Kenya I saw women who were nurses and doctors and teachers, and I started to think: If this woman can do it, why can't I? I began to realize how much a good education could bring to your life. The Kenyan women with educations were strong, they had a voice, they had equality. This was something I had never seen in my own culture.

I started to think that if I were educated, when I grew up I could take care of myself and my sister. I was about 13 then, and this was a whole new idea for me. I also knew anything could happen in Sudan, and that in the future I might be able to return. Whatever I learned in Kakuma, I could use back there. It would be good to have strong, educated women with equality and a voice when the war was over and Southern Sudan was rebuilt. So I started rushing through my morning chores and getting myself to school every day.

Sticking with my plan to be a strong, educated woman became much harder when I got to be fourteen or fifteen. That is the age when most Dinka girls from the countryside get married. City girls don't marry so young, so if my real parents had been with me, I don't think they would have wanted me to marry. But Deng, the man who was with Yar, was now my guardian. I called him my "uncle," and by custom he was allowed to negotiate with any man who wanted to marry me, asking for cows in exchange for his consent. A man in his late forties, older than my own father would have been, wanted to marry me and began coming to our house. My uncle would tell me to go sit with him, and the old man would tell me that he liked me. I was always honest, saying that I was not ready to get married. But he would try to convince me, saying all these nice things about me.

I also heard that other men were talking to my uncle about

taking me as a wife. Now, among the Dinka, a man can abduct a girl when she is walking alone, and then she has to marry him. So I was very, very careful, always surrounding myself with my friends when I was out and about. Sometimes I would even stay with a friend at night because I was afraid my uncle would make me go with one of these potential husbands.

This kept going on, over and over for two years. But during that time I also met John. He told me his name the first time I met him at a dance, and later he got up the courage to come and stand outside my house. Some girls saw him and yelled, "Look, there's a man standing by the gate." I peeked out of a window and thought, what does he want?

John

I remember exactly where I saw Martha for the first time. Some Lost Boys were teasing her and acting mean on the way home from school, but she ignored them. I thought she showed great courage. When I saw her later at that dance, I asked very politely if I could talk to her, which was a sign that I liked her. She turned me down in the polite way that all Dinka girls turn down all Dinka boys when they try to strike up their first conversation. Dinka tradition said she could not encourage me—or, at least, not right away. I would have to be persistent. So I started going to her house. She never told me she disliked me, so I thought I had a chance with her. I was determined to be her boyfriend. Day after day, I kept politely asking for her time. She kept saying no, but she always let me come back the next day. After many, many days, she finally said yes, she would allow me to visit her and we could be boyfriend and girlfriend.

Martha

John and I would sit and talk together. That is how "dating" is done in the Dinka culture. The man comes to your house, where you are chaperoned, and sits across the room from you, and the two of you talk.

Since John was a Lost Boy and I was a Lost Girl, we had a lot of background in common. He was a nice guy who seemed strong and confident, with no fear of anything. And he was young. I liked him, but I had more important things to think about just then.

That older man was still hanging around and hanging around. It got so I had to plan my whole life around avoiding him. My uncle kept telling him, "Oh, she's going to change her mind," or else, "If you find her alone, just take her."

A good friend of mine named Mary had gone through the same thing. Her uncle at Kakuma had wanted her to marry an older man, but her mother hadn't. So her mother ran away from the camp with her children. She took them to a secure place the

UN had, and they took her and her kids to Nairobi, the capital of Kenya. After that, they were able to emigrate to Canada.

I got a letter from Mary telling me that now she was free. No one could force her to get married. "I don't want to get married, and I can stay unmarried," she wrote. That sounded really good to me. She also told me to try to get to Nairobi, so we could speak by phone (there were no phones we could use in Kakuma). Also, once I was in Nairobi, she could wire me some money. Now that her life was better, she wanted to help me.

I found a family from Kakuma who was going to the city on the bus, and I went with them. Nairobi was overwhelming to me, bigger than any place I had ever seen. And it was so beautiful, with the shops, the tall buildings, the lights—electricity everywhere—and all the cars honking and streaming through the streets. It was so, so exciting. I had seen pictures of big cities, but I had never thought I would be walking around in one. This was a different world, a world I wanted to have.

Mary had wired me $200 so I could pay for my expenses and buy things I needed. I bought clothes for myself and my sister and even some for other members of our foster family. All too soon, though, I had to go back to Kakuma, and to the old man still waiting there to marry me.

I didn't want to marry that older man for a lot of reasons. I was already responsible for two people, myself and my sister, and I didn't want more responsibility. I had seen other girls get married, and their situation became even worse than the one I was already in. They worked all the time and had kids right away, even though they were just kids themselves. It was a depressing life.

Some of my friends thought I should get married, though. Traditionally, all Dinka women marry because it gives them a sense of belonging. But I wanted something else. I had been to Nairobi, and I had seen women who had educations and their own careers. I didn't have to marry, at least not now, not when I was so young. After all Tabitha and I had been through, all I wanted was to make a better life for us.

I had heard about Lost Boys going to America, so I asked a friend of mine who was a coordinator among the boys how that worked. He explained that if a boy wanted to go he filled out an application, and then he had to wait and see if he was accepted. "But what about the Lost Girls?" I asked him. "Can you find out if there's any way a girl can apply?"

He did this for me, asking an American woman who was a social worker at Kakuma. And her answer amazed me. She didn't even know there were Lost Girls! She thought the girls in camp were all living with their parents. She didn't know we were living in foster homes, where our guardians could marry us off for cattle or treat us almost like their servants. Girls in foster households took turns doing all the chores—some fetching water, others cooking or cleaning or scrubbing clothes by hand. The foster mother didn't have to do much. That's how it was in our household. We girls did most of the work. Again, part of that was just Dinka custom. Women were supposed to educate young girls—to teach them all these household chores. Yar had always taken good care of us, and she was trying to do what was right for us, but she was not our mother. If she had been my mother, she might have encouraged me to go to school instead of work so much. And she would have tried to protect me from the older man who wanted to marry me. I knew I would have to protect myself from that.

I asked my friend the Lost Boy coordinator where I could find this social worker so I could talk to her about the Lost Girls. He said I should go to the UN compound, just outside Kakuma. It was very hard to get in there unless you had a good reason to give to the security guards who protected the compound. But I went and waited and waited in a line at the gate. After I had been there almost all day, I finally got to the guards and told them I wanted to go in and talk to the white woman who was working to get Lost Boys to America. But they said, "No, you can't go in," and sent me away.

That night I told my Lost Boy friend what had happened, and the next day, he came to the compound with me. He explained to the guard that he was a coordinator for the Lost Boys and that the woman inside had asked to see me. Finally, around three o'clock that second afternoon they let us in and we found the social worker.

She was in a meeting, but she came out and asked what was wrong. She thought I was one of those women who had come to the compound because they didn't feel safe, because they thought they were going to be forced into marriage. There was a place for them to stay right next to the compound. But I explained, in my broken English, that I had come to tell her about the Lost Girls. My friend also helped me explain that I had heard about the Lost Boys going to America, and that some of us girls wanted to go there, to be educated instead of being forced into marriage.

She said that the program had been specifically set up for boys because no one even knew the situation of the girls at the camp. I realized in talking to her that we had been invisible.

But this lady was nice, she was listening hard to me, and she said she would get things fixed quickly for the Lost Girls. Then she asked if I was in any danger and if I needed to stay at the compound. Even though I was very afraid that my uncle would make me marry the older man, I couldn't stay at the compound. There would be no way for me to get Tabitha out of the foster home if my foster parents found out I had escaped from the camp. Tabitha was reaching maturity, and I knew that soon men would be coming to ask to marry her, too.

So I went back home, and in a couple of days, my Lost Boy friend gave me two applications to go to America—one for me and one for Tabitha. I was really pleased the social worker lady had done what she said and acted so quickly. I filled the forms out in secret so my foster parents wouldn't know—and with no high hopes. It was too much to wish for. But after about three weeks, I was called for an interview.

Soon other Lost Girls found out they could apply to go to America. Some of them didn't think it was a good idea, because they didn't want to leave their friends and the culture they knew to go to a strange land. But when I told Tabitha that

I was trying to get us to America, she wasn't afraid. Whatever I was doing was fine with her. I was getting really excited. I just wanted to get away. I was running away from marriage.

Within the month, I found out that our applications had been accepted. We were escaping, going to a place called America. That was about all I knew about it—and that we could get an education there and no one would force us to marry. I didn't even know that most of the people there were white.

Once we were accepted, we had cultural orientation courses, with movies and books that had pictures of America. Americans also explained to us about American culture—about not getting into physical fights (people in the camp fought all the time, sometimes even women and girls). They also told us how to interview for a job and how you should explain what a good person and hard worker you were. That was shocking to us. It seemed immodest. A lot of things were shocking to us. We were really excited, but we realized it was going to be very different in America.

Tabitha and I had to sneak out to these courses, because now I had to be very careful around my foster parents. If they found out I was leaving, they would surely try to marry me off before I could escape, so they could get the cows that man would give them for me. To try to throw them off my plan, I told them that, yes, maybe I would be willing to marry this man the next year. And I began being very nice to him, just trying to keep things calm until I could get Tabitha and myself away from Kakuma.

When I knew that we had been accepted to go to America, I told John. He was surprised and wanted to know why I hadn't told him before that I was applying. "Oh well, you know I didn't know that it would be successful," I explained. "I don't talk about things that I don't achieve." I saw a little concern in his eyes because I was leaving, but I couldn't allow myself to care about leaving anything or anybody in Kakuma. Still, I was hoping that he would be one of the Lost Boys who would come to America. I was happy when he said, "Oh, maybe I will join you. Maybe soon"—even though he didn't know whether he would be able to or not. "Good, maybe you will see me there," I said, but coolly. Dinka girls never give men too much encouragement. That is just how it is in our culture.

Really, I wasn't thinking too far ahead, about anything. I was just escaping from the situation I was in, and America seemed to be our only option. After all, it was supposed to be good.

But what if it turned out to be bad? Where would we go next?

John

In 1999, when I was twenty-four years old and Martha was sixteen, the U.S. State Department decided to allow certain refugees from the Sudanese civil war into the United States. The UN agreed with the decision. It said Sudanese children without parents could not be safely sent back to Sudan.

Interviewers from the outside world began coming to Kakuma. They represented social service agencies in the United States and the United Nations High Commissioner for Refugees. They began screening Lost Boys to see whether they had living relatives in Africa, and whether they had fought in the war. In either of these cases, you were not eligible for their program. About 3,600 Sudanese passed the interviews and began being processed for relocation to America.

One American interviewer who spent a year screening refugees at Kakuma said those who had tried very hard to get a good education in camp seemed to have survived with better mental health than those who had not. "Because they can see a way forward for themselves, they didn't lose hope," the interviewer said.

I was invited to apply to go to the United States. A refugee resettlement office called the Joint Voluntary Agency opened a file on me, took my picture, and scheduled me for an interview. I had to write my life story and give it to the interviewers. They asked me lots of questions, trying to see if they could catch me saying something that conflicted with my written autobiography. They knew that some refugees were so desperate to get to America that they would tell lies.

I had no trouble with the questions. I kept saying the same things over and over because those were the things that had happened. I told how I had lost my family the night the northern soldiers came to Duk Payuel, and how I fled across Sudan with Abraham. I told of how many people had tried to kill me, but that I had never become a soldier for the SPLA. I told of my years in Pinyudu and Kakuma. And I truthfully said I knew of no living relatives.

That was all very good. The interviewers said that I had passed, and they sent me to get a medical checkup. All the doctor could find, besides my being extremely thin, was a case of malaria. That could be kept in check with medicine, so the doctor sent me on my way to a final interview with the U.S. Immigration and Naturalization Service.

I had trouble following everything the interviewers said, but fortunately a translator repeated everything in Dinka. I learned that if I went to America, the government would take care of me for ninety days. My apartment, groceries, and utilities would all be free. After that, I would have to get a job and pay for everything. I did not stop to tell the translator or the interviewers that I did not know what apartment, groceries, and utilities were. When we were all done, the interviewers told me I would get a letter at the compound of the UN High Commissioner for Refugees in about two months telling me whether I had been accepted for relocation to the United States.

Believe me, when the letter came in May 2001, I was very happy. "You have been accepted," it said. I did not know exactly where or when I would go, but I did not care. I was going to America!

I began taking classes on how to be an American. I learned many of the things that American children learn in school, as well as some things they pick up at home. For example, I learned how to use a telephone. Perhaps the biggest surprise was learning about cold weather. A teacher told me, "I will show you how cold it gets in America." He pulled something out of a box and showed it to me. It looked like glass, only it had rounded edges like a river rock. He put it in my hand, and the rock burned the skin with intense cold.

"That is water," he said. "It gets so cold in America that water sometimes turns hard. We call this an 'ice cube.' Feel it, and feel the cold in America."

I had never seen ice. I could not imagine a country where water turned to stone. But I was aching to go there.

Part Six

PEACE

Martha

The day we left Kakuma forever, I had to sneak away from my old life. I told my foster parents that I was going to visit a friend in the camp for the day, and I explained to Tabitha that she needed to leave after I did and meet me at my friend's house. We each took just one extra outfit, hiding it under our clothes so our foster parents wouldn't notice.

When Tabitha got to my friend's, we left right away and hurried to the UN compound. A lot of Lost Boys were gathered to leave as well, and six of us Lost Girls. The UN people led us out to a plane that was very small and hot. We felt cramped in it, and very scared. I had never been on a plane before. As it began to lift off the ground, I looked down on all the Lost Boys gathered around the runway to say good-bye to us. Once we got higher, I couldn't look out the window, I was just too frightened. The plane kept lurching down suddenly, as if it would fall out of the sky. I was so, so happy when we were back on the ground again. But an even longer, harder flight lay ahead of us.

We knew we had to cross a great huge body of water, an ocean, and some of the Lost Boys said the water could pull the plane down into it. But when the time came, we walked up the ladder and into that the big plane anyway. We were going to try to get to America, whatever it took. There was no going back now.

In fact, this flight was okay, and the food was good, even though we didn't really know what went with what. We ate the bread and butter separately, ate the dry lettuce leaves, and drank the little container of salad dressing. And after a while, I dozed off to sleep, but every time there was turbulence, I would jerk awake, thinking the plane was falling out of the sky and into the ocean.

When we got to John F. Kennedy Airport in New York, about 30 of us Lost Children got off the plane, relieved but not knowing exactly where to go next. Suddenly we came to these stairs that moved and we didn't know what to do. We were scared to go down on them, and some of the boys said that these stairs were there to take people to a grinding machine, to grind us up. They were probably the same boys who said the ocean could pull a plane out of the air. After we stood there for a while, we finally decided we had to go down. Each of us stood in front of the moving stairs for a few minutes before we had the courage to step on. We thought we would miss our step and fall.

Tabitha and I and two other Lost Children, a girl and

a boy, were headed for Seattle. On December 19, 2000, our plane landed there. We had made it! It had been a long, long trip away from the Africa we had known all of our lives and to a new set of foster parents in America. We were tired and anxious when we stepped into the airport waiting area, but there to meet us was a group of people holding a big cardboard sign that said: "Martha and Tabitha, Welcome Home."

These people seemed excited to see us, and they gave us each a little wrapped box with a gift of earrings. We were astonished but so tired that we couldn't quite take it all in. Except for one Lost Girl in this group, everyone else was white. Amazingly, two women I had known at Kakuma were there. One was the social worker I had told about the Lost Girls, and another was the woman who interviewed us about coming to America. The rest of the people were our new foster family—Karen and Kirk Brackebusch, and their children Kyle, Christopher, and Kara, and another foster daughter, the Lost Girl whose name was Teresa.

We got into the Brackebuschs' van and drove out of the big city and away from the lights of Seattle that seemed to slash at the car windows. We were going to our new home—a smaller town in the countryside called Duvall. Our days-long journey finally ended at a house that seemed huge to us, with a big open kitchen and dining area with windows all around that let the outside in. To Tabitha and me the inside of the Brackebusch house felt like a large open field, not like a house at all. We were used to Dinka houses—all enclosed with just a little crack or door to let air in. We felt lost inside that house.

We just stared and stared, trying to understand it all.

It was Christmastime, so there were lights and decorations everywhere and a big tree inside the house, glistening with ornaments. That seemed amazing, too. So many new things to adjust to. Would we be able to?

As the days went by, things got better and better. When Christmas Day came, my foster mom's other family members gathered and there were another 50 people in the house. It was fun, and all the people were nice to us. They taught us games and gave us gifts. I felt very, very excited. We were finally with a loving, warm family. Somebody in this big group was always asking how we were doing and hugging us and taking care of us. When you feel that love for the first time, people caring about you, it's a wonderful feeling. No one had treated us like this since we had lost our parents. Finally, I could relax. Things were going to be okay.

After the holidays, we started school. It was cold, and we had to get up early in the dark. High school was not like the Brackebuschs' home at all. I was the only black person there. I felt like an odd person, and Americans seemed to close off from me. I confess I didn't reach out to them either. I didn't know the language or customs well enough, and anyway, I was too shy. I spent my time at school alone.

I'm used to white people now, but then they all looked the same. It was hard to learn the names of people and put them together with faces because all I saw was white. Also, it was hard to understand English because Americans seemed to speak through their noses, with a humming sound.

The classes were really hard for me, too. I took English literature and health and American history. But I had no connection to the history I was learning. It wasn't anything I had ever heard about before. And trying to follow classes taught in English was just plain hard. Reading went slowly, slowly, so doing homework was overwhelming. Everything I had to do every minute of the day was new—the culture, the schoolwork, the customs.

Then a strange thing started happening. All the emotions I had covered up before began to surface. Maybe it was because I had let down my guard a little for the first time since I was six. Now I could go to bed without worrying that somebody was going to come shoot Tabitha or me. At first that felt like a great relief, like a big weight lifting from my shoulders. But then I began having nightmares—people shooting and running, all the things that had really happened—and I began feeling very down. I tried to get over it, thinking it would go away, but it didn't. I think the dark, gray days of a Washington winter didn't help my mood much. I found myself crying a lot. Finally, I told my foster mom how I was feeling. She was a good woman, and she asked other foster parents how their Lost Children were doing. It turned out that a lot of them were going through this. Happily, Tabitha wasn't. She didn't have the memories I did, so she wasn't traumatized by them.

My foster mother began arranging weekends at her house where other Lost Girls in the area would come. There were about eleven of us, and we would listen to music together and braid each other's hair and cook Sudanese food. Socializing had been such a big thing in Kakuma. We had always been with other girls. Getting together again and reliving some of our past helped us a lot.

Slowly, I began to feel better and get used to life in America. I was even back in touch with Yar, my foster mother in Kakuma. She had learned where we were and written a letter explaining that when she first heard we had escaped to America, she had been worried that we were being taken into slavery. But now she had heard of other Lost Children doing well in America and she was relieved, knowing we were okay.

I managed to graduate from high school, and I began taking classes to be a nurse. While I did this, I supported myself by being a nursing assistant in a nursing home. Some of the people there were pretty cruel to me because I was a black person and they weren't used to that, but others were very kind.

Tabitha was still in high school, and she was finding the same thing. Some of the kids made fun of her because she was different. But she was feisty and tough, so she kept going and graduated from high school, too, a few years after I did. Then she started working and going to school at the community college.

Just before I turned twenty-one, I moved out of my foster parents' house and in with two friends—one a Lost Girl and another an American. I finally had a place of my own! It was exciting, but from month to month we worried about how we would pay for the rent, the groceries, and anything else we needed.

During those first years in America, I had been in contact with other Lost Kids who had left Kakuma and come to the United States. One of them was John.

Even though we Dinka people had had to leave our homeland in Southern Sudan years before, we had managed to keep our connections going through a kind of Dinka "grapevine." It helped that our names identified our clan and the area we were from. When I first got to America, I had gotten a call from some of John's cousins who lived in Texas and who had heard through the Dinka grapevine that I was in America. John had told them about me, and following Dinka custom, they had called me to continue the connection, telling me that John was still planning to come to America and that he was a good man and that he really liked me.

John

Refugees accepted for immigration to America kept watch on a camp bulletin board. Lists of names were regularly posted, and refugees could learn when they would leave and where they would go. I always rushed to check the new lists. Even if my name was not on it, I wanted to see which of my friends might be leaving soon.

The day my name was posted, my life changed forever. I was thrilled to learn I would be heading to an American city called Syracuse, New York. But that was just the first surprise. The second came when I looked around at the crowd of people near the bulletin board. I saw a man holding a big video camera on his shoulder. A second man carried a second, smaller camera. A third man stood nearby and seemed to be in charge of everything they did. He asked questions of the refugees gathered around the bulletin board while the first two men shot video. I did not know who the men were. I thought maybe they were from the American government.

I introduced myself to the man in charge. He turned out to be an American documentary filmmaker named Christopher Quinn. As I started to turn away, he asked if he could interview me on camera about my going to America. I agreed. I answered everything he asked, and when I went back to my hut, Christopher and the film crew followed me.

Thus began an association that lasted several years. Christopher filmed my preparations for traveling to the United States, along with those of two other Lost Boys. He followed us as we said goodbye to our friends and boarded a plane for New York. And he followed us for several months afterward, as I settled into Syracuse and the other two boys adjusted to life in Pittsburgh. The result of his work was a documentary film, *God Grew Tired of Us*. Through that movie and a book of the same name, lots of Americans got to learn about the Lost Boys for the first time. I was glad to be a part of that film and book because of what they did to raise awareness about Sudanese refugees. Eventually, the film prompted many viewers to give money to help the Lost Boys still in Africa.

I arrived in Syracuse in August 2001. All I had with me were the clothes I wore, a few photographs, my official immigration papers, and fourteen cassette tapes. I had tape-recorded the voices of some Dinka elders at a going-away party. They gave me advice on how to succeed in America, yet cling to my Dinka ways. I did not have a tape player. I figured maybe I could earn some money and buy one in America. I certainly did not have any money on me. I didn't even have a dime in my pockets.

Nothing I had learned in Kakuma had prepared me for the fast pace and richness of life in America. My first glimpse came at JFK Airport in New York City. There were huge crowds of people going in every direction. And they all moved so quickly! I made my way to a connecting flight and landed in Syracuse. A group from my sponsoring church met me outside the terminal and drove me to an apartment I would share with other Lost Boys. There were several Lost Boys in Syracuse, and I made new friends. I also had friends from my new church, who helped us settle into our apartment and our new lives.

I began working right away. I worked several jobs during my first year in America, sometimes two or more jobs at once. I worked in a factory, at a fast-food restaurant, and at a parcel shipping center. I eventually got my best-paying job, as a nighttime security guard at a hospital. Meanwhile, during the day, I got an associate's degree from Onondaga Community College and began work on a degree in public policy at Syracuse University.

I had never given up hope that I might one day reconnect with my family. Though it seemed likely that they had died during the shelling of Duk Payuel, I never actually saw their bodies. While I was in Kakuma, I had written letters to the International Red Cross, asking for help in finding my family. I had no luck while I was in Africa. However, things began to change after I settled in Syracuse. I wrote letters to my friends who were still in Kakuma. I told them about my having arrived safely in America and about my new life. One of my friends in Kakuma got to leave camp and spend some time in the nearby country of Uganda. He told people he met about his friend John and his new life in America. That story got picked up and spread by other people. By sheer coincidence, the story eventually reached a man named Goi. My friend and Goi met, and Goi asked about John in America. My friend gave Goi the name of my clan, the Bor Nyarweng.

Little did he know that Goi was my brother. On that tragic night of noise, confusion, and darkness in Duk Payuel, I had run one way, and the rest of my family had run another way. They walked to Uganda to get away from the fighting, going south as I went east with Abraham. They had all survived.

Goi told our mother, "I found a man who talked about a Nyarweng named John today. He said John is alive."

"No," my mother told Goi. "John is dead."

Goi had hope. He and my brother Aleer decided to contact me. Aleer wrote me a letter. I got it on October 18, 2002.

"John," Aleer wrote, "if you are my brother, please, can you write to us? And if you are not my brother, please throw this letter away. . . . If you are my brother, we are still alive —mother, father, and all of your brothers and sisters, plus a sister born after you left, named Akuot. Unfortunately, our three uncles were killed in the shelling, along with their families." Aleer gave a few details about how they had ended up in Uganda and closed with his phone number.

I could not believe my good fortune. After fifteen years of believing my family had died, I would soon be talking with them. One of my friends gave me a plastic phone card to pay for long-distance calls, and I used it to call the number Aleer had given me. In Uganda, Goi answered the phone and handed it to Aleer. After only a few seconds, the connection was cut. Silence. No matter what I did, I could not re-establish the line. It was 1 a.m. I decided to wait until dawn, when it would be twilight in Uganda, and tried the call again.

Once again I spoke with Goi and Aleer. We shared our stories. I told them of my years in refugee camps and how I had come to America. Goi and Aleer started crying. I cried too. But my mother refused to speak to me. She refused to believe I was her son. She thought I was dead and that some impostor was trying to pull a cruel joke, or that Goi and Aleer were lying to her to make her feel better. They could not convince her to talk to me, so I had to hang up the phone.

Two days later, I tried again. I spoke again with Goi and Aleer. This time they got my mother to put the receiver to her ear.

"Mother, this is John. I am the one."

"No," she said. "You are not my son. . . . If you are my son, tell me the other names I used to call you."

Every Dinka mother has a secret name or two for her child. I remembered mine. I said, "Did you call me Makat? Did you call me Runrach? Did you call me Dhieu?"

Makat means "born when people are running away," Runrach means "bad year," and Dhieu means "cry." My nicknames referred to my being born during a bad year when two of my father's brothers died in a raid. There was silence on the other end of the phone for a moment, and then my mother knew the truth.

"It is you! But your voice seems different," she said.

She last had seen me when I was thirteen. Here I was now, nearly thirty. "I'm now a grown man," I told her. "Today, I'm tall."

We talked some more, and I decided to send her some money. After that, we talked at least two or three times every week.

I started a campaign of phone calls and e-mails to get my mother to come to join me in the United States. After two years, I won the battle. My mother and little sister flew to Syracuse in February 2004 to live with me.

So life settled down for me in America. And after so many years of despair in East Africa, things started to look up there, too. While I was a student at Syracuse University, I set up a foundation to help improve the lives of Sudanese refugees still in Africa, as well as Lost Boys who had moved to America. I began speaking publicly about the plight of the Lost Boys and Lost Girls. With many of my new American friends helping me, I raised enough money to open a medical clinic in Duk County, where I grew up. It is the first medical facility of any kind in Southern Sudan.

Life was so much better, but not quite complete. For all of the blessings I had received, there was one I still yearned for. I wanted to marry Martha.

Martha

One day in 2001, I got a call from John's relatives in Texas saying he had just arrived in America. I told them to call me back when he was settled in and I would call him. I had a lot of things going on then, as I tried to make the adjustment to America, but I followed through on my promise. I called to welcome John. He was all the way on the other side of the country, but he kept calling me. We had many long conversations, and over the phone we got to know each other again. John seemed like a good man, a very responsible man. After about a year, he came to Seattle to see me. After a couple of years of phone conversations and visits, I agreed to marry him. That meant a lot of negotiating began back in Sudan.

John

I knew I wanted to marry Martha in the Dinka manner. She agreed, but there were many details to work out. My father, back in Africa, arranged for a marriage dowry of cows. I would have to pay some cows to people representing Martha's family before I could marry her.

JOHN

Martha

Through the Dinka grapevine, I knew I had an uncle, my mother's brother, in Kakuma, even though I had never met him. Since I had no father to represent me, my uncle became the person that John's family in Sudan had to negotiate with. After many months they agreed to a dowry. Normally, the husband's family would give the wife's family a dowry of cows, but in this case, John agreed to send money worth the equivalent of eighty cows. In the winter of 2005, once the dowry was settled, we were considered married in the eyes of the Dinka tribe.

John

B y then, my mother and sister were living with me, and my mother spoke no English. I convinced Martha that moving my mother across the country would have been difficult for her. Martha agreed and moved to Syracuse. Her sister, Tabitha, came later, and we moved into a new house with my mother and sister.

Martha

When I got to Syracuse, John's mother and sister cooked for me for the first few weeks, to welcome me to the family. That is Dinka custom. New brides don't cook at first. After those first weeks were over, there was an official day when I cooked and we had a celebratory meal with other Sudanese friends. If I had had female relatives of my own, they would have helped me prepare the feast, but instead other Dinka women came with food. My status as a Dinka wife was now official.

We decided to have an American wedding, too, at the First Presbyterian Church of Skaneateles, outside Syracuse. The members of this church had sponsored John to come to America and had helped him so much.

On June 2, 2006, the church was filled with our new American friends and with Lost Boys and Girls from all over North America. Even Mary, my friend in Canada, who had helped me make my first visit to Nairobi, was there. It was a day of great celebration and dancing, in American and Dinka style.

The wedding was exciting, but the most exciting day for me was when my daughter, Agot, was born. A daughter I could take care of and make happy seemed to heal some of my pain at having lost my own childhood. But things were about to change even more.

Late at night in November 2007, the phone woke me up. When I answered, I heard the voice of a cousin I had reconnected with—a Lost Boy now living in Sydney, Australia. His voice sounded excited, and he began to explain that he had been at a church service in Sydney, a church that other Dinka people also attended. When new visitors were asked to introduce themselves, a man stood up and said that he and his wife had just come to Sydney from Egypt and that their name was Akech. The man said, "We just keep praying that we will connect with our daughters, who were lost years ago." The man said he knew that some people at the church came from Kakuma, and he thought they might have heard something about two little girls on their own. My cousin recognized the man's name—it was his uncle!

After the service, he walked over to introduce himself to the couple, and there was a big reunion right there, with his aunt breaking into tears and hugging and hugging him, her lost nephew, her sister's son. Finally my cousin broke the big news. He knew where the lost daughters were! They were in America!

I held the phone in my hand, listening to his voice, but I just couldn't take it all in. It was as if my mind was numb, as if

I'd had a good dream that I would wake up from. I had to keep touching my arm, testing to see if I could feel, if I was really awake. We had always been hoping to find our parents, but I had almost given up that hope.

The next month I flew to Australia with my new baby and reunited with the parents I hadn't seen for more than twenty some years. My father came to the airport to meet this daughter who was now a woman, with a child of her own. He didn't even know how to recognize me. Any young woman walking off a plane with a little girl could have been me. But he found me, and I found my parents.

We spent a month getting to know each other again, and I discovered that I had a brother and a stepsister. I also discovered what I had lost years ago in that village in Southern Sudan: a parent's love. Your own mother and father are full of this natural love for you. You can feel it, and with them you can feel at home, secure, taken care of, loved no matter what.

Now as I go through my day, I know I have parents, and that changes everything, even if they're on the other side of the world. I'm a parent, too—with three children now—and that changes everything as well. For so many years, I was a Lost Girl, but I'm not lost anymore.

John

R emember how I said that we Dinka are storytellers? As Martha and I get our children ready for bed, I tell them many stories from Southern Sudan. I want them to understand their culture and the ancient roots of their family.

Sometimes I tell them of my father. When he was young, he became famous as a wrestler. People knew his name far and wide, and they respected his talent. He had a thick chest and powerful arms and legs, and he could throw any man to the ground. He went from village to village and defeated every local champion. The Dinka admired him as much as any American sports fans look up to an athlete who scores a touchdown or hits a home run.

But my father had another side, and not everyone knew about it. He liked to sing songs just for fun. He would make them up as he worked, and he sang them beautifully. Eventually he gave up wrestling and became a well-respected judge. But he never stopped singing.

When I introduced myself to people when I was young, I said I was the son of Deng Leek. They often gasped in surprise and delight and said, "You are the son of the man who was the great wrestler!" But my wrestling career was not meant to be. I grew up very, very skinny. I did not have the muscles of my father. Still, people thought I might grow strong someday. They hoped I might keep the family tradition alive.

I never did grow as powerful as my father. But like him, I became a very good singer. I made up lots of songs, and my singing made people happy. One day, my aunt made me an ornamental Sudanese bracelet of sinews and low cow hairs. Many Southern Sudanese men wear such bracelets to show they are stylish and manly. The tufts hang down, and when you dance with a girl you flick your arm and make the cow hairs move. We say it is like flashing your cow's tail. My aunt thought it would look good if I flicked the bracelet while singing.

"Now that you know how to sing a song, will you not be a good wrestler like your father?" she asked me.

I said, "I will do both."

And I have. I have not fought men like my father, and I have not become a professional singer. But I have fought many, many times to stay alive, and I have won that wrestling match every time. I am blessed. Today, living in America, I sing my new song of joy and hope.

Afterword

As I look into the future, I see so much more work I can do to help in Southern Sudan. The civil war finally ended with a comprehensive peace agreement between the north and south in January 2005, just about the time Martha and I were married. Life in Southern Sudan began to return to normal—or as normal as can be after a war that killed more than 2 million people and forced millions of others out of their homes forever. But of course there is still an enormous amount of work to do to bring prosperity back to Southern Sudan.

In addition to the clinic, I also have plans for opening something called the Southern Sudan Institute. It will combine a school for agriculture, a peace and reconciliation center, and a library. To stock the library, I already have received donations of thousands of books from a charity called the International Book Bank. The reconciliation center will promote peace, and the agricultural school will teach people how to cultivate crops. Those who were born after the start of the civil war in 1983 probably did not get much education about how to grow food and need to learn that skill scientifically.

I do these things because I have benefited so much from my life in America and I want to share that goodness with my homeland. I want to help make a better future for Southern Sudan and particularly for the Dinka.

I have gotten a lot of help from many generous Americans. Christopher Quinn's film won a major prize at the Sundance Film Festival in 2006 and appeared all over the country in movie theaters the following year. Many who saw the movie donated money, volunteered time, or otherwise helped ease the suffering of the Lost Boys and Girls. The executive producer of *God Grew Tired of Us* and his wife gave my foundation a big donation. I did not know who they were when I met them, but I do now: American actors Brad Pitt and Angelina Jolie.

Selected Timeline of Sudan

1956: Sudan becomes an independent nation. The government pushes Islamic rule that the southern tribes are against.

Late 1950s: Civil war begins when the north tries to stop a southern rebellion by burning villages.

1969: Southern Sudanese continue to revolt, fearing the government will make Sudan a Muslim country.

1972: Northern and Southern Sudan reach a compromise with help from the United Nations and the World Council of Churches.

1973: The Socialist Republic of Sudan is formed. The south becomes self-governing and the north makes Islam the state religion.

Late 1970s: Southern Sudan's self-governing begins to fall apart.

1983: A second revolt begins when the north begins a policy of rotating soldiers between the south and north. Southern soldiers do not want to leave their families. A Muslim legal code is put into place.

1984: The Sudan People's Liberation Movement announces it will bring down the government with help from the Sudan People's Liberation Army (SPLA). The SPLA attacks northern army and government stations in Southern Sudan, resulting in open warfare.

1987: Northern armies raid John's village. John flees.

1989: Northern armies raid Wernyol, the village where Martha and Tabitha are staying with family. The two little girls flee.

1992: The forces of Sudan's ruling government begins the largest offensive of the long civil war.

December 19, 2000: After years as refugees, Martha and Tabitha arrive in the United States.

2001: Negotiations begin between the SPLA and the government in Khartoum.

August 2001: John arrives in the United States after years of life as a refugee.

2005: A peace agreement ordering a permanent cease-fire is signed. Humanitarian organizations begin helping to bring hundreds of thousands of refugees home.

May 2007: John Dau opens the Duk Lost Boys Clinic in Southern Sudan where thousands of Sudanese receive lifesaving medical care.

To all of the other lost children in the world, whose stories have not been told —kmk

To the spirit of Sudan —ms

Published by the National Geographic Society.
All rights reserved. Reproduction of the whole or any part of the contents without written permission from the National Geographic Society is strictly prohibited.

The National Geographic Society is one of the world's largest nonprofit scientific and educational organizations. Founded in 1888 to "increase and diffuse geographic knowledge," the Society works to inspire people to care about the planet. National Geographic reflects the world through its magazines, television programs, films, music and radio, books, DVDs, maps, exhibitions, live events, school publishing programs, interactive media and merchandise. *National Geographic* magazine, the Society's official journal, published in English and 32 local-language editions, is read by more than 35 million people each month. The National Geographic Channel reaches 310 million households in 34 languages in 165 countries. National Geographic Digital Media receives more than 13 million visitors a month. National Geographic has funded more than 9,200 scientific research, conservation and exploration projects and supports an education program promoting geography literacy.
For more information, visit nationalgeographic.com.

For more information, please call 1-800-NGS LINE (647-5463) or write to the following address:
National Geographic Society
1145 17th Street N.W.
Washington, D.C. 20036-4688 U.S.A.

Visit us online at www.nationalgeographic.com/books
For librarians and teachers: www.ngchildrensbooks.org
More for kids from National Geographic: kids.nationalgeographic.com

For information about special discounts for bulk purchases, please contact National Geographic Books Special Sales: ngspecsales@ngs.org. For rights or permissions inquiries, please contact National Geographic Books Subsidiary Rights: ngbookrights@ngs.org

Library of Congress Cataloging-in-Publication Data
Dau, John Bul.
Lost boy, lost girl : escaping civil war in Sudan / by John Bul Dau and Martha Arual Akech ; with Michael Sweeney and Karen Kostyal.
   p. cm.
ISBN 978-1-4263-0708-9 (hardcover : alk. paper) -- ISBN 978-1-4263-0709-6 (library binding : alk. paper)
1. Dau, John Bul--Juvenile literature. 2. Akech, Martha Arual--Juvenile literature. 3. Refugees--Sudan--Biography--Juvenile literature. 4. Sudan--History--Civil War, 1983-2005--Juvenile literature. I. Akech, Martha Arual. II. Title.
HV640.5.S9D39 2010
962.404'3--dc22
[B]   2010017960

Cover design by Jonathan Halling. Interior design by Mark R. Bacon & David M. Seager.
The body text of the book is set in Hoefler Text. The display text is set in Bourgeois.

Illustration Credits:
Cover: Background photo, Gerry Ellis / Minden Pictures. Artwork by Jonathan Halling.
Insert: All photos courtesy of the authors, unless otherwise noted below:
Dinka village, Paul Almasy / Corbis ; Boy Milking cow, Wendy Stone / Corbis ; Refugees walking, Wendy Stone / Corbis Sygma ; Lost Boys, M.Amar / UNHCR
Spot Art: David M. Seager

Printed in the United States of America
10/WOR/1